MARLON SAUNDERS

Foreword by Kenny "The Jet" Smith
2x NBA Champion/Host of "Inside the NBA"

LIFE IS LIKE SPORTS

HOW TO TRIUMPH *OVER* LIFE'S OBSTACLES

LIFE IS LIKE SPORTS:
HOW TO TRIUMPH OVER
LIFE'S OBSTACLES

Marlon Saunders

DIXON
PUBLISHING COMPANY

Dixon Publishing Company
P.O. Box 32023
Aurora, CO 80041
DixonPublishingCompany.com
facebook.com/CeneceDixon
twitter.com/CeneceDixon

The publishing midwife is a division of Dixon Publishing Company, LLC.
The Publishing Midwife and logo are trademarks of Dixon Publishing Company.

Dixon Publishing Speakers Bureau provides a wide range of authors for speaking events.
To find out more, go to DixonPublishingCompany.com or
Inquiry@DixonPublishingCompany.com.

Dixon Publishing Company books may be purchased in bulk for business
educational, or promotional use. For information, please contact
your local bookseller or the Dixon Publishing Company Distribution Center
DistributionCenter@DixonPublishingCompany.com.

Interior book design by Michael Myers, Dixon Publishing Company
Managing Editor, Felicia Ransom, Supreme Documentation
ISBNs: Paperback: 978-1-966684-10-7
Hardcover: 978-1-966684-11-4
Ebook: 978-1-958735-39-8

Printed in the United States of America

Table of Contents

Dedication

"The man who finds a wife finds a treasure, and he receives favor from the Lord." Proverbs 18:22 (New Living Translation)

"Let your wife be a fountain of blessing for you. Rejoice in the wife of your youth."
Proverbs 5:18 (New Living Translation)

This book is dedicated to the love of my life, my heart, my beautiful wife of over 20 years, the wife of my youth, Tamara, who has spent every day loving, supporting, praying, and pushing me toward the potential she saw in me when we first met. I never believed one could marry their best friend until I met you. God gave me the right one and the perfect one when He gave me you. Your presence in my life is proof of God's overwhelming love for me. I love you!

"Children are a gift from the Lord; they are a reward from him. Children born to a young man are like arrows in a warrior's hands."
Psalm 127:3-4 (New Living Translation)

This book is also dedicated to our three amazing children, Mason, Sydney, and Maxwell, who will never know the indescribable joy they have brought and continue to bring to my life. Being your dad has been one of the greatest honors and privileges I have ever received. I am so proud of you three and love you more than you will ever know.

Tamara, Mason, Sydney, and Maxwell—the four of you keep me constantly wanting to outdo yesterday's version of myself.

Foreword

Throughout the years, Pastor Marlon Saunders has helped me in so many ways spiritually and emotionally. I am elated that I am now afforded the opportunity to return the favor to a small degree with this foreword. I have always felt refreshed and renewed after hearing Pastor Marlon's sermons, especially those that pertained to sports.

I was blessed to have a stellar basketball career. High school All-American, college player of the year and a two-time NBA champion. The lessons learned inside each of those journeys also had a personal spiritual impact; learning to be comfortable in uncomfortable environments and learning that doing the ordinary things extra can make you extraordinary.

I always credit Pastor Marlon Saunders for showing me how to connect all of that to a higher power. I thank him for that.

I hope this book inspires you as he has me. To my avid Lakers Pastor, (my only issue with him) may this book bless others but also bless you!

Kenny "The Jet" Smith
NBA Expert Analyst
Host of Top-Rated Emmy Winning Show "Inside The NBA"
2x NBA Champion (Houston Rockets)
Nine Seasons in the NBA
Kenny Smith Entertainment Group

Acknowledgements

First and foremost, I acknowledge and give all glory, honor, and praise to my Lord and Savior Jesus Christ, without whom I would literally be nothing. Without Jesus Christ in my life, I would be completely lost. Every gift, talent, and ability that I have is solely the result of Jesus' grace, mercy, and unconditional love being present and active in my life. This book would not exist without the presence and leading of Jesus Christ. I owe everything that I do to Him.

I want to express my deepest and most heartfelt gratitude to my dad and my mom, Jim and Swanzi Saunders. Without you, not only would I not be here physically, but I would also not have the spiritual, emotional, and psychological base needed to accomplish God's purpose for my life. My spiritual nature is a direct result of the spiritual nurture you both provided me since my birth. The most important thing any parent can give a child is a relationship with Jesus Christ. You gave me that and I will forever be grateful.

I would also like to express my deepest love and thanks to my father-in-law and mother-in-law, Trelles and Marcia Stepter. You have given me the greatest gift I have received since Jesus, your daughter and my wife, Tamara. You have also been another set of parents to me. Your priceless love, support, prayers, and unwavering belief in me have never and will never go unnoticed and unacknowledged. You will truly never know what you both mean to me. God gave me the best in-laws ever and I am eternally grateful to have you in my life.

I would like to say thank you to the church that Tamara and I launched in 2008 in Valencia, California, Valencia Christian Center. Thank you for the many years that you allowed me to serve and develop as a Senior Pastor, leader, and visionary. So much of what I do now, I learned through trial and error with you.

I will never have accurate or enough words to express my endless, indescribable, and most overwhelming love, gratitude, appreciation, and heart for the congregation of Hope City Church of Colorado. You have given me my hope back. You truly put the "family" in the phrase "church family." From our initial service on Sunday, April 23, 2023, where over 750 of you showed up, to now, where over 2,000 of you locally and over 3,000 of you nationwide call Hope City Church of Colorado your church home, I have never and will never be able to describe what you mean to me. You all hold a special place in my heart that I did not even know existed. Thank you for living up to your name, not just in my life, but in the lives of countless others. You are truly a God-given, God-assigned, precious, and priceless family that has left me speechless and in awe of what God can do with a people committed to serving Him and each other.

There is truly, "no place like Hope."

Thank you to the best manuscript editor ever, Felicia Ransom. Your long hours, hard work, constant and consistent prayers, motivation, ideas, thoughts, feedback, wisdom, editing expertise, professionalism and commitment to excellence truly made this entire experience easy, enjoyable, and fulfilling. Here is to the first of many books that you will be editing for me.

Thank you to my incredible publisher, Cenece Dixon. Your prayers, encouragement, calm voice giving insight and direction, knowledge, and wisdom regarding how it all works were exactly what God knew I needed to get this book done. Your constant push to keep going was priceless and motivated me to keep writing no matter how I was feeling. I thank God for you! Thank you for moving me forward in this project one text or phone call at a time.

Thank you to my absolutely amazing photographer, Jaymie Alexander. You have come through for me, Tamara, and our entire family on countless occasions. From the numerous promo photos, family photos, Christmas photos, church photos, and now book cover photo you have solidified your place in our hearts and home. Your vibrant personality, smile, love, care, and concern for how we are represented through photos always brings the perfect energy to capture exactly what is needed for the moment. Keep those batteries charged because we are just getting started.

Thank you to everyone who has shown unwavering and unconditional love and support for me throughout my entire journey. Your prayers and encouragement have truly motivated me to continue journeying toward being the best me that God created me to be. I remain immensely grateful and full of love for you all. Finally, thank you to all of you who hold this book in your hand whether it is physically or digitally. You have expressed support in a very tangible way. Your possession of this book fills me with encouragement, hope, joy, and a sense of purpose that brings indescribable gratefulness to my heart for you. I acknowledge that a book can be great but without support from people like you, it remains a great secret. Thank you for helping ensure this book is not a secret through your love and support. I pray that your investment will produce a priceless return that proves to be exactly what you never even knew you needed.

Introduction

Excited, grateful, overwhelmed with hope and joy for what this book will produce in your life, does not even begin to describe how I feel.

This book has been in the making for quite some time. What began as one Super Bowl Sunday sermon years ago titled, "Life Is Like Football," gradually transformed into a personal quest to explore a variety of sports in hopes to uncover practical and spiritual principles that we all could apply personally with the goal of maximizing our lives on every level.

The original sermon, "Life Is Like Football," was intended to draw people to church on Super Bowl Sunday morning and impact them in such a way that as they watched the game later that day, they not only experienced it differently, but felt the principles conveyed from the sermon that morning solidify in their hearts and minds. The feedback received was so overwhelmingly positive that I decided to teach another sport-themed sermon during baseball's World Series. As you may have guessed that sermon was called, "Life Is Like Baseball." Before I knew it, I was exploring sport after sport and soon developed a sermon series titled, "Life Is Like Sports."

While I do have my favorite sports, there are a few sports that I never really viewed or studied closely, yet after doing a deep dive into observing those sports, they serve as a source of some of the most powerful and impactful lessons that I have ever applied to my life.

My prayer is that you not only savor each sport-infused chapter you read, but you also consider how each sport is relatable to your life. I pray that each sport will present a set of truths and tools that will play on throughout the rest of your life. I pray that you receive everything you are desiring and needing to enhance your life whether you were conscious of it or not. Sometimes the greatest blessing is receiving something you never knew you needed. I pray that God will do "…exceedingly abundantly above all that [you] ask or think" (Ephesians 3:20b – NKJV) as you read this book.

All the motivation, inspiration, revelation, and illumination needed for and contained within this book is a direct result of studying the strategies and methods that Jesus Christ employed in His earthly and public ministry as He attempted to connect with His wide range of audiences. Regardless of the individual background or belief system, Jesus had an indescribable and priceless way of communicating with people. He had a very practical and identifiable approach that helped people comprehend the life-giving spiritual and practical principles that He was seeking to convey. He would often couch these principles in metaphors and parables. His parables were everyday real-life stories that the listener could relate to and draw an understanding from regardless of education or experience.

As the listener was able to relate to and understand the metaphor or story being told, they were also able to glean the practical and life-enhancing application that served as Jesus' ultimate goal.

Life is Like Sports: How to Triumph Over Life's Obstacles aims to have the same effect. The intention and purpose behind this book are to find common ground for all of us, regardless of cultural, social, economic, ethnic, or historical differences, through the universal and timeless activity of sports. Then, use this common ground to convey spiritual and practical truths that will result in life-enhancing clarity, understanding, wisdom, knowledge, and strategy.

The first six chapters of this book were part of the sermon series, "Life Is Like Sports" that I taught in church. The remaining eight chapters have been written exclusively for this book.

May God richly enhance, empower, and edify your life as you remember and uncover powerful and impactful truths behind these everyday sporting events.

Chapter 1
LIFE IS LIKE FOOTBALL: HOW TO BE POSITIONED FOR SUCCESS IN LIFE

"Finally, be strong in the Lord and in his mighty power. Put on the full armor of God, so that you can take your stand against the devil's schemes. For our struggle is not against flesh and blood, but against the rulers, against the authorities, against the powers of this dark world and against the spiritual forces of evil in the heavenly realms. Therefore, put on the full armor of God, so that when the day of evil comes, you may be able to stand your ground, and after you have done everything, to stand. Stand firm then, with the belt of truth buckled around your waist, with the breastplate of righteousness in place, and with your feet fitted with the readiness that comes from the gospel of peace. In addition to all this, take up the shield of faith, with which you can extinguish all the flaming arrows of the evil one. Take the helmet of salvation and the sword of the Spirit, which is the word of God. And pray in the Spirit on all occasions with all kinds of prayers and requests. With this in mind, be alert and always keep on praying for all the Lord's people."
- Ephesians 6:10-18 (New International Version - NIV)

I will never forget the life-changing revelation that I experienced one year as I watched the NFL football games, leading up to Super Bowl Sunday. My perception changed as I intently gazed at the football games, no longer seeing them as just sporting events or forms of entertainment. Suddenly, the lens from which I viewed the games changed. While the natural aspect was most certainly still there, the games began to take on a far deeper meaning for me. The more I observed, the more I was impacted on a level that I had never experienced before. Various aspects of everyday life began to flash before me while viewing the games. My mind began alternating between football and real life, and it was not long before I realized that life is like football.

I quickly discovered that football has many spiritual aspects, being a wonderful source of Christian symbolism and reflecting so many of the struggles that we face in our spiritual lives. Consider the need for constant conversions, the presence of opposing forces, the setbacks those forces can cause, the need for a playbook and the wisdom that it gives, the need for a quarterback and the dependence on him, the need for a constant huddle with the quarterback, the fears of being overcome by your opponent, and that's just to name a few.

Imagine it is football game day, focusing your attention on the football field and stadium, you immediately notice that most of the people are in the stands criticizing and talking about what they would do and which way they would have run had it been them on the field. Some are commenting, "You can't see that open hole," or "What is wrong with you?" "Oh, he can't play; he keeps getting tackled; take him out of the game." The sad reality is, too many of us will not participate in the game of life and are far too comfortable critiquing from the stands. I believe God would say to many of us, "Instead of judging what everyone else is doing from the stands, why don't you get in the game yourself?" It is easy to criticize from the stands and hypothesize about what we would do and could do. However, none of it matters unless we suit up and partake in the game ourselves.

In viewing the football field, you observe that it has boundaries. Those boundaries are designed to keep you in the game. You cannot grab the ball and run up to the stands, knocking popcorn out of everyone's hands. You must grab the ball and play according to the rules that are connected to the game. Too many of us do not like the rules set by God and do not like God's set boundaries. However, the boundaries are designed to keep you in the game. I do not think it is mere coincidence that every ten yards you get the first down and at the same time, God has given us the Ten Commandments to keep our lives moving forward and progressing in His perfect will. It would be great if we all paid attention to the Ten Commandments like football players pay attention to the ten yards.

As we get out of the stands and understand that God has placed boundaries in our lives to effectively advance us in this game of life, it is important to understand that just like in the game of football, it matters how you suit up. It matters what gear you wear. The right gear is everything!

THE RIGHT GEAR

In football, the gear that is worn is crucial. You cannot run out onto the field decked in anything you desire. Having no gear or the wrong gear will result in major injuries. Can you imagine running out on the football field and attempting to play in regular clothes? Not good! Too many of us attempt to play and press through life's obstacles without the gear that God has given us, and we wonder why we experience so much injury, so many setbacks, and so many traumatic and tragic situations. Oftentimes, it is because we attempted to play without the proper gear.

The question becomes, "What is the proper gear for success in triumphing through life's obstacles?" In Ephesians 6:10, God gives us a list of gear that we must put on to gain victory through life's battles.

Ephesians 6:10 states: "Finally, be strong…" Success in this life requires a certain amount of strength and you are not alone. "Be strong in the Lord and in His mighty power." In other words, trust who God made you. The scripture continues: "Put on the full armor of God, so that you can take your stand against the devil's schemes. For our struggle is not against flesh and blood, but against the rulers, against the authorities, against the powers of this dark world and against the spiritual forces of evil in the heavenly realms." Considering this scripture, you must understand that your ultimate problem is not a particular individual, but rather the spirit operating inside of that individual. You attack people when you need to attack the spirit inside of the people. The problem is not your boss. The problem is the spirit inside of your boss. We do not fight against each other. We fight spirit versus spirit. That is the reason you must learn how to take a restroom break every now and then at work. Go to the restroom, close the door behind yourself and say, "I come against that spirit in the Name of Jesus. You will not destroy my Monday! You will not spoil my Tuesday!" The solution is not another email. The solution is "knee-mail." The Bible affirms in Proverbs 3:6: "In all your ways acknowledge Him, and He shall direct your paths." (New King James Version – NKJV). Therefore, we must learn how to progress through prayer. Have a conversation with God and allow Him to direct you safely into overcoming whatever it is or whoever it is trying to come against your peace, patience, and perseverance.

Ephesians 6:13-18 (NIV) states: "Therefore put on the full armor of God, so that when the day of evil comes, you may be able to stand your ground, and after you have done everything, to stand. Stand firm then, with the belt of truth buckled around your waist, with the breastplate of righteousness in place, and with your feet fitted with the readiness that comes from the gospel of peace. In addition to all this, take up the shield of faith, with which you can extinguish all the flaming arrows of the evil one. Take the helmet of salvation and the sword of the Spirit, which is the word of God. And pray in the Spirit on all occasions with all kinds of prayers and requests. With this in mind, be alert and always keep on praying for all the Lord's people."

Notice that there is no gear, no weapon, for your back. Why? Because God never intended for you to run from the enemy. He intended for you to defeat the enemy and cause him to run from you.

Apostle Paul, the writer of Ephesians said he is giving you seven things that you must put on. He said the first thing you need to do is make sure that you have "The belt of truth buckled around your waist." In a very practical sense, your belt does not just hold up or cover key areas, it gives you security. Spiritually speaking, the belt of truth also provides security, security for your life. You are more secure when you walk in truth. Just because you do not go to the mailbox does not mean that you do not have any bills. Truth! If you are just authentic to yourself, you never have to remember who to be. Walk in truth.

Apostle Paul said the next item that he wants you to place on after you put on your belt is the breastplate of righteousness. In football, this would be the pads that protect your chest. However, spiritually speaking and practically speaking, this is something that will protect your heart. For many of us, our heart is always broken because it is always left either unprotected or unproperly protected. We must put on the breastplate of righteousness to protect the heart that God has given us. What does that mean practically? That means that we guard our hearts with boundaries and standards based on living in truth, forgiveness, love, integrity, obedience to God, personal spiritually and biblically based beliefs, and purpose-driven thinking. When we create these types of standards and boundaries around our hearts, our hearts become a protected organism that is not easily accessed or broken and we become more apt to open our hearts to individuals who have proven that they operate in accordance with the standards and boundaries that we have placed around our hearts. For instance, someone who has shown that they do not operate in truth does not gain access to our hearts. The "gates" around our hearts can be unlocked with the key to truth and other standards and boundaries that the "gates" are made from.

In addition to putting on your belt and your breastplate, Apostle Paul proclaimed you must put on the shoes of peace. In football, this would be your cleats. However, spiritually speaking, this is the foundation of peace that God makes available to us through having a relationship with Him. This God-given peace helps us to stand firm and walk with confidence, faith, and hope. This is the peace of God that comes through having peace with God. Peace with God comes through having a sincere relationship with Him. The peace of God will help you dig in and stand with God during the storm.

Now that you have put on your belt, breastplate, and cleats, you must put on the shield of faith. In football, this would be the arm pads. When a football player is running, this is the first piece that goes out against the opposing player. The opposition contacts this before he contacts anything else. Spiritually speaking, this is your faith. The enemy contacts your faith before he contacts anything else. You must have your "arm pad" (your faith) out there so that when the enemy comes against you, he comes against your faith. Despite the opposition, your faith, like your peace, is what makes you dig in and keeps you grounded and focused on moving forward. Your faith helps protect your heart. Your faith reminds you that no weapon formed against you is going to prosper. Your faith is what makes you boldly declare that your peace and joy will not be destroyed. Your dreams and goals will not be destroyed. Your family will not be destroyed. Nothing that pertains to your spiritual or natural well-being will be destroyed because you have a faith that helps you do the seemingly impossible.

Apostle Paul is still not done with the list. After putting on the belt, the breastplate, the cleats, and the shield, he said that we must put on the helmet of salvation. In football, the helmet provides protection for your head and your brain. Spiritually speaking, Apostle Paul is talking about protecting your mind.

Your mind is the most powerful weapon that you possess. Everything starts with your mind. All your external actions are the result of the thoughts that you have and hold within your mind. Every battle is first won or lost in your mind before it is won or lost in a natural, physical, or tangible way. Nothing just happens. Thoughts and habits are birthed and given life in and through your mind. That is the reason the Bible gives clear instruction on the types of thoughts that we should hold and constantly replay in our mind. The Bible declares in Philippians 4:8: "Finally, brothers and sisters, whatever is true, whatever is noble, whatever is right, whatever is pure, whatever is lovely, whatever is admirable— if anything is excellent or praiseworthy—think about such things." (NIV)

Being that your mind is your most powerful weapon, it must be guarded. You must protect what you allow to flow in and out of your mind. It is important to remember the words of the Apostle Paul in 2 Timothy 1:7: "For God has not given us a spirit of fear, but of power and of love and of a sound mind." (NKJV). Understand that God has already given you a sound mind. It is a gift from God. As with any gift, it is our job to do what is needed to keep the sound mind that God has given us. Our spiritual enemy makes it his job to try and steal our gift. The enemy is hoping that somehow, he can get you to exchange your sound mind for a chaotic mind, depressed mind, confused mind, or unsettled mind. Having a sound mind means having a right mind. God has given you your right mind. Having a right mind, at its core, means having a mind that is constantly trusting God and finding peace in His presence, protection, and provision. Philippians 2:5 declares: "Let this mind be in you which was also in Christ Jesus." (NKJV). This means constantly possessing a victorious mindset, an overcomer's mindset, a winner's mindset, understanding and living encouraged in the fact that every test leads to a testimony, and believing that somehow God is going to turn your biggest mess into your biggest life's message. When you know, understand, believe, and walk in this, it becomes easier to embrace the much-needed ongoing transformation of your mind by the constant renewal of your mind as declared in Romans 12:2.

Unbelievably, the Apostle Paul is still not done with the list. After putting on the belt, the breastplate, the cleats, the shield, and the helmet, he expresses that we need to pick up the sword of the Spirit. In football, which is the playbook. In football, this gives you all the directions, instructions, and strategic plays that you need for success. Spiritually speaking, this is our Bible. It is important that we learn to strategize by using the Word of God. All the instruction and direction that we need can be found in the Bible. Every response, every adjustment, everything required to continue moving forward in life, despite the opposition, can be found when we open and study the Bible.

After mentioning the belt, the breastplate, the cleats, the shield, the helmet, and the sword, Apostle Paul then gives us the final piece of equipment needed for triumph over life's obstacles. He says that in addition to those things, we need prayer. In football, this would be your jersey. Why? Your jersey functions as your final and ultimate covering. Your jersey, in many ways, brings it all together to function as one unit. Spiritually speaking, that is exactly how prayer operates in your life. Prayer functions as your ultimate covering. Prayer covers every area of your life because as you talk to God, He shows you exactly how to use every piece of "equipment" that He has gifted you with. Prayer unites everything. Prayer causes everything to work together. Prayer makes it all make sense. Whatever you do, pray first. Again, the Bible states in Proverbs 3:6, "In all your ways acknowledge Him, and He will direct your paths." What does it mean to acknowledge God? It simply means to include Him by recognizing that He is present. I have discovered that recognition brings revelation. In other words, when I recognize God, He reveals His next steps for my life to me. Prayer is merely a conversation with God. It does not have to be long or deep in meaning. It certainly does not have to be in the King James Version or using words that are incomprehensible. It is simply an open, honest, and transparent conversation with God. He loves when you are just you. Have a conversation with Him today and watch how much clearer things become.

When you are fully geared up with your belt, breastplate, cleats, shield, helmet, and sword, you are ready to play. When a football player is fully geared up, he can bounce back after a major hit. He can bounce back after being tackled. Why can he bounce back? He has completely covered and protected himself. When you completely cover yourself spiritually by walking in truth, guarding your heart, firmly planting your feet, being led by your faith, covering your mind, and starting everything with prayer as you take notes from the Word of God (your playbook), just like a football player can bounce back, you can bounce back from anything!

THE RIGHT TEAM

When it comes to discussing the teams on the field, first notice the fact that there are only two teams present. Spiritually speaking, there are only two teams that you can be a part of in this game of life – God's team and the devil's team. Contrary to what some may believe, you cannot play for both teams. I cannot say that I play for God's team on Sundays and the devil's team (which would be the team of the world that operates contrary to God's Word) Monday through Saturday, except for Wednesday Night Bible Study.

In football, it is important to understand the role of the quarterback. Spiritually speaking, God is our quarterback, and just like the quarterback on the football team, God is always in the game with you. You never have to play by yourself. God's Word promises that He will never leave us nor forsake us. In football, the quarterback calls the plays because the quarterback often sees what other players cannot see. The plays for the team come through the quarterback who is using the playbook to give direction. In life, all our "plays" come from God as we allow Him to quarterback for us. What makes it even better is that God is not just familiar with the playbook, but He wrote the playbook (2 Timothy 3:16). Imagine having a quarterback who wrote all the plays based on His knowledge of the opposition. That is exactly who God is and what God has done for us.

In football, every regular play begins with the football getting into the hands of the quarterback. Practically speaking, the football represents our destiny, and it starts in the hands of God. Certainly, other players, from the punt return receiver to the center, touch the football before it gets into the hands of the quarterback. For us, this just signifies the fact that God will allow us to see and get a feel of our destiny at distinct stages of life, however we must always make sure to put it back into His hands.

Observe how plays are executed. The center takes the football and kneels forward as he is getting into position to hike the ball to the quarterback. It is worth noting that the defensive player directly in front of the center, known as the nose guard, does not get into position until the center gets into position. Know that the devil, your spiritual enemy, does not get into position until you get into position, and know that his entire job is to stop you from moving forward. That is the reason it can seem like the harder you try sometimes, the more opposition you have, but do not worry about that because you have the ultimate advantage. You have God as your quarterback.

THE RIGHT PLACE

Perhaps one of the biggest lessons I have ever learned from football came when I actually paid close attention to how the quarterback passes the ball as the team executes the play. The center snaps the ball and while the offensive line is blocking (those are God's angels dispatched to protect us), the receivers run to the places where they were instructed to go. The quarterback then throws the ball to the receiver in that place. Whatever you do, do not miss this point right here. It is important to know that the quarterback does not throw to the player, but the quarterback throws to the place. In life, God does not throw our destiny, blessings, or favor to wherever we are. He throws it to where He told us to go. Provision falls when you get in the proper place. In Genesis 22, we see the story of Abraham and how God helped him exercise and grow in his faith by instructing him to sacrifice his son Isaac. Well Abraham did not have to go through with that. Thank God because that would have scarred several people for an eternity. There was a "ram caught in the thicket by its horns" (Genesis 22:13) but notice that the ram did not show up when Abraham agreed to obey God. The ram showed up when Abraham walked in obedience and faith and got to where God told him to go. A great analogy would be to describe the doors of the grocery store. The doors at the grocery store do not open for you when you decide you are going to the store. They do not open for you when you get in your car. They do not open for you when you pull into the parking lot. They do not open for you when you park your car. They do not open for you as you are walking towards them. They open for you when you get into the right place at the right time. Once you get into the right place at the right time, the sensor picks you up and the doors open all by themselves. You do not need a key. You do not need to force them open. You do not need to break in. You just need to get into the right place at the right time. If you feel as if the blessings are not falling the way that they should, consider your current placement and ask God to help you make sure that you are where He told you to go.

THE RIGHT TIME

I learned that the quarterback will sometimes perform this action where they throw the ball extremely high, and it seems to take forever to come down. This is referred to as hangtime. I remember asking a friend of mine once, "Why does the quarterback do that?" My friend said, "He does that to give the receiver a chance to get to the place that he told him to go." The quarterback has vision that the receiver may not have. The quarterback can see the defense in spots where the receiver cannot see them. For this reason, what the quarterback will do is release the ball and give the receiver a chance to shake off the defense. This is exactly what God does with us sometimes. He releases our blessings, but they take longer to fall giving us a chance to shake loose everything that is trying to stop us. As a result of this, knowing that your blessing has already been released, keep running, keep fighting, keep shaking off opposing forces and keep pressing toward your future and the place that God told you to go knowing that at any moment, that blessing is going to fall right into your hands. Always remember that delay is not denial. Your prayer request has not been denied, but it may be delayed so that you can shake off everything that would try to instantly steal your blessing out of your possession. It is coming down, just keep going.

What I love most about this is that unlike the actual game of football, when God is quarterback, there is no interception. The enemy cannot steal what God has intended to give to you. You do not have to worry about an interception. What is yours is yours, period!

THE RIGHT SUPPORT

The final point that I learned about how life is like football is the cheerleaders! We dare not forget about the cheerleaders and the role they play in the overall game of football. The cheerleaders are there to encourage, motivate, and show unconditional support for their team. God has assigned some "cheerleaders" to us. We all have people who are believing for the best in us while constantly encouraging us, motivating us, and showing unconditional love and support towards us. Sometimes the cheerleader comes in the form of your Pastor. In some cases, the cheerleader comes in the form of a family member, or friend. Occasionally, the cheerleader is a co-worker or manager. Sometimes the cheerleader is a stranger. Rest assured that though they show up in many forms, we all have cheerleaders assigned to us. Embrace the support and use it as fuel for the journey.

Since that Super Bowl Sunday, I have never viewed football the same again. Neither have I seen life in the same fashion. It is a blessing how God can take everyday events and present life-enhancing principles. I thank God for football, but more than that, I thank God for showing me, and now you, how life is indeed like football, and how football equips us with practical and spiritual tools for success in how to triumph over life's obstacles.

A Moment of Reflection
Chapter 1: Life is Like Football: How to be Positioned for Success in Life

As you reflect on how "Life is Like Football," consider how you are currently positioned for success in life. Have you discovered any "gear" that has been missing from your life or any "gear" that needs to be strengthened? How does the idea of God being your "quarterback" influence your approach to life? What can you do to ensure that you are in the place that God has assigned for you? Can you remember an instance where God's delayed timing worked in your favor? What support do you currently have around you that you are grateful for?

A Moment of Reflection

A Moment of Reflection

A Moment of Reflection

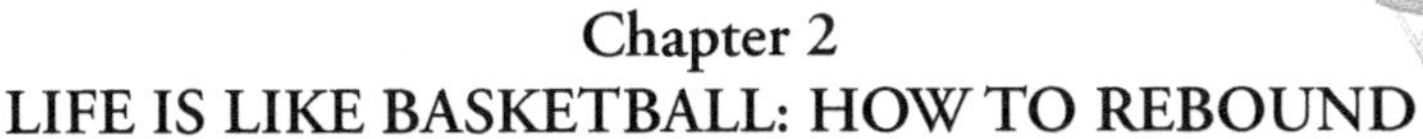

Chapter 2
LIFE IS LIKE BASKETBALL: HOW TO REBOUND

"So, David inquired of the Lord, saying, "Shall I pursue this troop? Shall I overtake them?" And He answered him, 'Pursue, for you shall surely overtake them and without fail recover all.' So, David went, he and the six hundred men who were with him, and came to the Brook Besor, where those stayed who were left behind."
- 1 Samuel 30:8-9 (New King James Version - NKJV)

In 1 Samuel 30:8-9, David wants to know if it is permitted for him to pursue a troop in an effort to get his possessions back. Have you ever had a simple desire to recover things that you lost? You are not alone. I have felt this way, many have felt this way, and that is exactly how David feels in this scripture. There are many of us who desire to recover some things but may not know exactly how to go about doing so. Perhaps you desire to recover something very tangible such as a car, home, money, or perhaps a career or relationship. It may be something intangible such as joy, peace, happiness, hope, or a sense of comfort. Whatever it is, I am here to tell you that you absolutely can recover whatever you have lost.

I could not see how to recover anything that I had lost until I paid close attention to the game of basketball. The more I watched basketball, the more I discovered the tools needed to recover things in my own life. It was when I paid particularly close attention to how players rebounded the ball that I discovered how to rebound in life. As we walk through the fundamentals of rebounding in basketball, you will discover how the same fundamentals are applicable to rebounding in life.

Before we get to the fundamentals of rebounding, it is worth reminding you that no matter how great a player is, no player makes every single shot that they attempt. The most outstanding player still misses their shot sometimes, so take the pressure off yourself and understand that in life, you may make some and you may miss some. It then becomes a question of, "Can you keep shooting?" Can you imagine a player who missed a shot and said, "Forget it, that's it, I'm never shooting again." We would all look at that player and say, "You are not serious, are you? You must keep shooting." At its core, basketball is all about who can make the most shots. therefore, in order to win, you must shoot. One way to ensure that you will not win is to decide to stop shooting. If you do not shoot, you will not score. If you do not score, you will not win. So, no matter how many shots you have missed, keep shooting. Let me make it truly clear, I do not care how many times you have tried something, and it did not work, keep trying. Do not give up. You have never failed a day in your life. If anything, you have discovered diverse ways in which something does not work, so, smile and keep going. Do not let a "missed shot" affect your confidence. You are still more than a conqueror! You are still a natural-born winner. You are still God's chosen one. You are still amazing!

Seeing that players often miss shots; the game of basketball also becomes a game of rebounding. When the shot is missed, can a team recover the ball? When your attempt at something is missed, or you feel as if you have lost something, can you recover? The answer, again, is yes, but the question is "How?"

There are five essentials to rebounding in basketball that will equip you with the mindset and game plan that you need to always recover and rebound in your life. Here we go! Imagine the basketball being whatever it is that you are trying to recover.

ASSESS

What does it mean to assess? It means to have a clear picture of what you are up against. It means knowing exactly what you are dealing with. You cannot overcome anything that you are not willing to face. You cannot overcome anything that you are in denial about. As I mentioned in the chapter about football, it is so important that we walk in truth. It is worth repeating what I said in that chapter; just because you do not go to the mailbox, does not mean that you do not have any bills. Too many of us have difficulty recovering simply because we are in denial and unwilling to deal in truth.

Great basketball players take time to assess what they are up against. Is the opposition bigger, faster, younger, and/or stronger? In addition to knowing the answers to those questions, you also need to know who is on your team. As you assess your life, have a clear picture of exactly who is on your team and who is not on your team. If nothing else, knowing that, helps you pass the ball to the appropriate people and keep the ball away from the erroneous people. Too many of us have passed our peace to people who are not on our team. We have passed our joy to people who are not on our team. We have passed our trust to people who are not on our team. We have passed our heart to people who are not on our team. Learn to recognize who is for you and who is against you.

As you assess your life, be honest about your income, your spending habits, your credit score, your qualifications, and skill set for potential jobs or job promotions, your time management habits, your personality, your relationships, your experience, your education, your history, and your overall approach to life. What motivates you? What are your goals? Before we can move forward in recovering things that we would like to recover, we must first do an honest assessment.

POSITION

Great basketball players will tell you that properly positioning yourself is key to being a successful rebounder. The distance between you and the player on the other team matters.

The stance that you are in while you are guarding the other player matters. The attitude that you have while guarding the other player matters. Your confidence matters. Your mindset matters. Your courage matters. All those things make a clear statement to the other player. In everyday life, all those things make a statement to both your spiritual opposition and your natural opposition. Your emotional, psychological, and spiritual positioning are the difference between overcoming and being overcome. Take time to ask yourself where you are in each of these areas and discover the health and effectiveness of your positioning. You must understand that properly positioning yourself in basketball starts long before the actual game. I discuss this in more detail in Chapter 4: Life is like Boxing, but basketball players will tell you that your eating habits, practice routine, and overall personal care is what lays the foundation for properly positioning yourself. As it is in the natural, so it is in the spiritual. Understand that your spiritual routine matters. It matters who and what you listen to. It matters who and what you let speak into your life. Reading your Bible matters. Having an active prayer life matters. It all lays the foundation for you to become properly positioned. If you are going to recover, you must properly position yourself spiritually before you do anything else. If your spiritual being is unhealthy, your natural being will suffer.

Let us move now to the free-throw line. These last three fundamentals come directly from the tools that players use to recover a shot coming from the free-throw line.

SPEED

While players are waiting for the free throw to be shot, they know that they will have to move quickly because moving slowly and casually does not help them. As simple as this sounds, too many of us are not recovering because we are not moving, and for those of us who are moving, we are not moving fast enough. Too many of us are sedentary and waiting when we should be moving. If you are going to recover, you cannot afford to sit around letting life happen to you. You must get moving and actively pursue your possessions. It is worth noting that the players who are waiting for the free throw to be shot rarely have the ball come directly to them after the shot is attempted. If they are going to retrieve the ball, it is going to be because they pursued the ball. Such is the same with life; nothing just comes to us. We must pursue what we want, and we must pursue quickly. Sometimes the biggest issue is that we have simply let feelings like frustration and discouragement keep us from actively and quickly pursuing what is ours. Pursue that career. Pursue healing in that relationship. Pursue financial health by pursuing your credit management and living on a budget. Pursue your education. Whatever it is, pursue it!

TIMING

While you must pursue quickly, you must pursue quickly at the right time. Timing is everything! Ecclesiastes 3:1-8 is all about being able to recognize timing. Players that are waiting for the free throw to be shot will tell you that if they pursue too soon, it is a violation and they have worked against themselves. If they pursue too late, then they do not stand a chance of retrieving the ball because it has already gone to someone else. While speed is all about moving quickly, timing is all about knowing when to move. For too many of us, we know exactly what to do, but we do not know when to do it. It is possible to do the right thing at the wrong time and miss an opportunity. If you are going to recover, you cannot move too soon or too late. For some of us, the window of opportunity is closing because we will not move. For others, the window is not yet open. When you pray, pray that God will reveal the right time to you. Here is a personal secret. Whenever I pray, I always ask God to make the answer so loud and clear, that it would be impossible for me to miss it, and guess what? He always does! Ask Him to reveal to you, your timeline. If you ask Him, He will answer.

BOX OUT

Boxing out is all about positioning yourself between the opposing player and the basketball hoop. To retrieve the ball, the player must decide to get in front of the other player and move them out of the way, clearing a path to retrieve the ball. Imagine your opposing player is doubt, bills, poor credit, relationship issues, health issues, or anything that is obviously working against you and attempting to keep you from owning back joy, peace, confidence, or happiness.

What you must do is learn how to get in front of those issues by "boxing them out." When you box them out, they no longer stand between you and your possessions. They no longer block your view. They are no longer an obstacle. They are officially behind you. You are no longer trying to get around them or through them to get to what is yours. They no longer block your path. They have become a non-factor. Learn how to quickly put negative things and negative people behind you and clear the path to pursue what belongs to you. Start by reprioritizing. You properly reprioritize by creating a list of the most important life-giving or positive things that you desire to have. You know you are prioritizing properly when your list supports your peace and not people's opinions. You must manage everything or everything will manage you. Be very deliberate about how you manage every aspect of your life. Create a management game plan. You are always one game plan away from a life-changing solution. What is your game plan for managing what has been managing you? Strategize by creating a list. After you create your list, "box out" or block out anything that is not helping you achieve what is on your list.

It is worth noting that when a player is boxing out another player, they are not staring at that player. They are boxing that player out, but their focus is on the ball. Their eyes are on the ball. In life, it is easier to box things out when you stop gazing at them, allowing them to negatively monopolize your mental space, take a positive approach that controls them, and shift your focus from that to your goal. Stop focusing on what people are doing and saying and use that energy to focus on what is really important, your happiness.

Let us use credit as an example. If you are trying to rebound in your credit, you must "box out" all the negative and self-defeating things like feeling overwhelmed to the point of doing nothing or making comments like, "I'll never be able to fix this." Box those things out and focus on your ultimate goal. Always remember that victory comes one step at a time much like a basketball game is won one basket at a time. Do one thing today that moves you in the direction of victory. You may not be able to pay off an entire bill today but do something. Perhaps that something is a minimum payment toward that bill, or a phone call that sets up payment arrangements toward that bill. Box out the negativity by doing one thing that moves you toward your eventual goal. Every positive step is a step in the right direction.

SECURE

Every player knows that once they get the rebound, the opposing player is not going to waste any time trying to stop them from moving forward. The opposition is going to be right there in their face. Knowing that, what does a smart player do? They secure the ball. They ensure that the ball cannot be easily taken from them. You must know that once you make progress and you recover what is yours, your spiritual enemy is not going to waste any time trying to steal it from you again. The enemy would love to steal your joy again; therefore, you must set things in place to secure what is yours. We cannot be so excited to recover that we become irresponsible. Celebrate responsibly. Whatever God places in your hands becomes your responsibility to protect. Take ownership of everything that God has given you, whether physically, spiritually, emotionally, or mentally, and refuse to let anything or anyone steal it out of your possession. Secure your stuff. Place boundaries around your blessings. Take the steps necessary to never again lose what you have had to regain.

With that being said, know that things lost are often regained. Whatever you feel like you have lost, know that you can get it all back. Assess the situation, get properly positioned, move quickly, move at the right time, box out, get your stuff back, and secure it. Rebound!

A Moment of Reflection
Chapter 2: Life is Like Basketball: How to Rebound

As you reflect on how "Life is Like Basketball," is there anything that you feel as though you have lost that you are looking to recover or restore? What essential(s) given in this chapter impacted you the most?

A Moment of Reflection

A Moment of Reflection

A Moment of Reflection

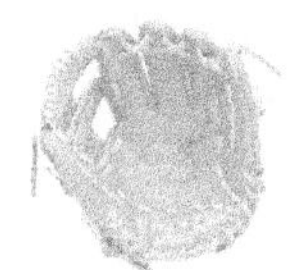

Chapter 3
LIFE IS LIKE BASEBALL: HOW TO HIT A HOMERUN

"Not that I have already attained, or am already perfected; but I press on, that I may lay hold of that for which Christ Jesus has also laid hold of me. Brethren, I do not count myself to have apprehended; but one thing I do, forgetting those things which are behind and reaching forward to those things which are ahead, I press toward the goal for the prize of the upward call of God in Christ Jesus."
- Philippians 3:12-14 (NKJV)

Various observations are seen in the scripture noted above. The Apostle Paul makes the statement that he is focused on one thing. He says, "But one thing I do." Too many of us cannot seem to make effective and lasting progress because we are not focused on one thing. We are trying to do everything. You are most effective when you narrow down your goal and focus on the one thing you would like to see happen.

Also notice that the Apostle Paul declares, "Forgetting those things which are behind." I believe that the only time we need to look back is to see how far God has brought us and to make sure that we are not repeating unhealthy cycles. You cannot drive a car forward looking through the rear-view mirror. Therefore, you cannot move your life forward if you are always looking back. The past is gone. Maximize the present while preparing for your future. Focus forward.

The final observation to focus on is when the Apostle Paul states, "I press toward the goal." The question becomes, "How do I press forward?" "How do I position myself now to have a successful future?" The answer to this question is found in baseball; specifically, what it takes to position yourself for a home run in baseball. You will discover that the same thing that it takes to position yourself for a home run in baseball is the same thing that it takes to position yourself for a home run in life.

In baseball, the goal is to get on base. The goal is to score. In life, the goal is to make progress, be productive, and produce or accomplish something that has lasting results.

You were not created to lose. You were not created to "strikeout." You were created to conquer. You were created to win. The issue that many of us have is that we simply do not know how to conquer, or how to win.

If you were a baseball player, it would be important that you understand that you may not hit the ball every time you swing. You most certainly will not hit a home run every time you swing. However, you must keep swinging. As you keep swinging, you get better, and you get smarter. As you are getting better and smarter, your hitting percentage increases. In life, you will have great days and not so great days. You will have days when it feels like you can conquer anything and days where it feels like anything can conquer you. That is just life. However, you must keep swinging.

Below are eight keys to positioning yourself for a home run in baseball and a home run in life.

DECIDE WHAT'S NEEDED

In baseball, if it is your turn to bat, you must know what item you need in your hands. A golf club will not work. A hockey stick will not work. You need a baseball bat. There is nothing wrong with the golf club or the hockey stick if you are playing golf or hockey. However, they are not the right equipment for the game of baseball. You will strike out attempting to use the right equipment for another sport. Too many of us are approaching life with the right tools for another journey. Your life's journey requires tools that are designed specifically to help you accomplish God's purpose for your life. That is the reason you cannot simply mimic another person's actions and expect optimum results for your life. At best, you become an impressive copy. For some of us, we have the right ideas for another life, or the right concepts for another scenario. Just because it worked for someone else does not mean it is your answer as well. It is important to know the difference between something being good and something being God. Something can be good for someone else, but not God's plan for you. God has placed us all on our own individual journeys. Those journeys require different resources, personalities, academic pursuits, career paths, and relationships. I pastor a church. While it is wise to see what others are doing, have mentors, accountability partners, ask questions, gather information, do research, and exchange ideas, it is not wise to simply assume that what may work for one pastor, will also work for me. We are two different pastors in two different cities with two different congregations and two different callings, purposes, and responsibilities. Our gifts and talents differ. Our personalities differ. Our communities differ. Our means by which we accomplish what God would have us to do differ. Therefore, I must ask myself, "What is needed for my journey?" Always tailor your needs list to your specific journey. What do you need a degree in? Where do you need to live? What conferences do you need to attend? What do you need for what God is calling you to do? As you admire the success of another, always remember that admiration should produce motivation, not duplication.

Now is a wonderful time to survey your life and ask yourself what is working for you and what is not working for you. Here is an effortless way to make that determination. Know that there are only two categories as it pertains to productivity. Things are either working for you, or they are working against you. Nothing is kind of working for you. Take a moment and ask yourself what things are working for you and what things are working against you. Once that list is complete, make an effort to eliminate everything that is working against you. Some of these things may be expensive or even painful on some level to release. However, releasing anything that is working against you is well worth it. It may be difficult today, but there is so much more peace and fulfillment waiting for you on the other side of the release.

DECIDE THE DETAILS FOR WHAT'S NEEDED

All baseball bats were not created equal. They vary in length, size, and weight. They also vary in use. There is a bat for fast pitch baseball and a bat for softball. There is also a bat for adult leagues and a bat for youth leagues. There are metal bats and there are wooden bats. Once you determine that you need a bat, your follow- up question is, "What kind of bat do I need?" In life, once you determine what you need, you must then determine the details to what you need. For example, if you know that you need to go back to school, the follow-up question is, "What do I need to go back and study?" If you know that you need to eat healthier, the follow-up question is, "What do I need to remove or include into my diet?" If you know that you need to change your friendship circle, the follow-up question is, "Who needs eviction papers from the circle and who needs an invitation into the circle today?" If you know that you need to manage your money better, the next question is, "What do I need to stop spending so much money on?" Once you discover that you need to change your circumstance, environment, scenario, or situation, the next question will always be, "What specifically needs to change about it?"

STEP UP TO THE PLATE

Even the most unmatched baseball player will tell you that no batter can hit the baseball from the dugout or the bench. All batters must step up to home plate as it is a requirement for any batter who desires to hit a home run. By stepping up to the plate, batters are getting into position. Many times, we are not "hitting home runs" in life because we refuse to "step up to the plate" and get into position. What does that mean? That means accepting responsibility and facing things head on; being deliberate and direct in our dealings, and not running from situations, but confidently approaching them with the mindset to knock it out of the park. Leaving the dugout or bench means leaving your comfort zone. Just like a batter must leave the bench and walk up to the plate, many of us need to leave the couch and walk or drive up to the location that places us in position to hit a home run in life.

Once a batter walks up to home plate, they position themselves in what is called a "batter's box." There is a batter's box on the left side of the plate and a batter's box on the right side of the plate. Depending on whether the batter is a left-handed batter or a right-handed batter, they will determine which side of the plate they will stand on. The bottom line is, once they walk up to the plate, they choose a side. In life, we must select a side. What does that mean? That means we must stand for something. Too many of us are struggling to hit home runs in life because we are indecisive and waver. We do not want to hurt anyone's feelings, so we try to please everyone. We try to be everyone's friend. We become what the Bible labels as "lukewarm." We become so lukewarm that people cannot identify whether we even have morals or principles, and if we do, they have no idea what they are. There is no way to be all things to all people and remain your authentic self. You must stand for something, and you must stand with someone. In doing that, some people will get upset, but like my dad used to say, "It's ok, they'll be alright."

If you watch baseball, you will often notice that once a batter steps up to the plate and picks a side, they dig into the dirt with their cleats. This helps them get planted and stabilized. In life, once we engage a situation, we must be all in. We cannot expect to hit a home run if we are not fully committed. We cannot perform moderately and expect full results. We also cannot afford to be emotionally, mentally, psychologically, spiritually, or physically unstable. We must be rooted, grounded, and fully planted in every area of our approach. Being planted means being focused, confident, courageous, persistent, and consistent. Effectiveness and success begin with digging in and getting planted.

RELAX

A batter cannot hit a home run afraid, nervous, worried, or anxious. If a batter is going to hit a home run, the first thing they must do is relax. In life, we cannot maximize the opportunities given to us if we are constantly approaching life with fear-based emotions. The Bible states in Philippians 4:6 (NKJV), "Be anxious for nothing, but in everything by prayer and supplication, with thanksgiving, let your requests be made known to God." Matthew 6:25-34 discusses worrying and how it produces nothing. Too many of us cannot hit home runs in life simply because unhealthy or negative emotions are leading us. We are worrying too much; worrying must be overcome because worried or not, the ball is coming. Full of anxiety or not, life is happening. Therefore, we must do all that we can to overcome uncertainty. Sometimes the greatest tool used against us, both naturally and spiritually, is doubt or some fear-based emotion. Sometimes, people and the spiritual enemy are both hoping that you are too scared or apprehensive to go for the home run. The Bible gives a clear solution for those of us who find ourselves being governed by any fear-based emotion. The Bible instructs us to talk to God about it. Let God know that you are nervous and worrying and that you need His help to overcome that fear. Here is a quick sidenote about prayer. We do not pray to inform God (He already knows all about the entire situation – even aspects we are yet to discover), we pray to include God. Prayer is simply an action that makes the statement that I cannot and will not do this without God's help. If you are scared, nervous, worried, or anxious, talk to God about it and leave it with Him. Once you say, "Amen," start walking in faith that you have overcome all nervousness and concern. The more you pray, the more fear and anxiety will fade. Ultimately, you will discover that praying people do not worry and worrying people do not pray.

DON'T SWING AT EVERYTHING

An exceptional batter knows that not every pitch is the same. Just like baseball bats, pitches are different. They vary in speed, rotation, and pattern. Therefore, every excellent batter knows not to swing at everything, but rather wait on the perfect pitch for them. It is important to note that the perfect pitch for one may not be the perfect pitch for another. For instance, some batters can hit a curveball while others will strike out every time. In life, the baseball represents opportunity. Just like the batter knows that pitches are coming, we must know that opportunities are coming. However, just like the batter knows to wait on the pitch that is perfect for them, we must learn to wait on the opportunities that are perfect for us. Too many of us are so eager to prove ourselves to others or recover from a setback that we will "swing" at anything. We want to bounce back from a sour relationship, start a business, or show someone that we do not need them so intently, that we will go after every opportunity that comes our way. Not all opportunities are worth pursuing. There is a dramatic difference between a good opportunity and a God opportunity. We must possess the discipline to bypass what is good for the sake of pursuing what is God. Quick note, if it does not help push you into your God-given dreams and goals, then it may be good, but it is not God. Wait for what is God. Your God-given pitch. Your God-given opportunity. Proverbs 4:7 (NKJV) states, "Wisdom is the principal thing; Therefore, get wisdom. And in all your getting, get understanding." Whenever opportunities come your way, ask God to give you wisdom and understanding so that you can make the right decision and not just "swing" because it looked good.

FOCUS

Focus is everything. Many of us cannot reach our goals simply because we lack focus. We have the gifts, talents, abilities, and resources, but not the focus. Focus is what makes everything that we have going for us effective. Without focus, nothing else matters. In baseball, the defense will do whatever they can to interrupt your focus. However, a great batter stays focused on the ball regardless of the distractions. The ball is the priority; therefore, the ball must remain the focus. When you get focused, you become unstoppable. When you get focused, you can overcome anything. When you are focused, you can accomplish whatever you set out to do. When you are focused, you do not give your time or attention to anything that is not helping push you toward your ultimate goal. Light at its most focused point is a laser and a laser can cut through anything. When you are focused, you can push through anything. One concept that helps me focus is my constant belief that God is bigger than anything that I am facing. Instead of seeing my God through the eyes of my problem, I see my problem through the eyes of my God. When I do that, I know that God is still in control, and everything is going to be okay. The other element that helps me focus is remembering what the Bible declares in Philippians 4:8 (NKJV), "Finally, brethren, whatever things are true, whatever things are noble, whatever things are just, whatever things are pure, whatever things are lovely, whatever things are of good report, if there is any virtue and if there is anything praiseworthy— meditate on these things." I have learned that my focus is only strong when I entertain things in my mind that fall into one of the categories listed in this scripture. Finalizing your envisioned future is possible when you stay focused.

STRIKE AT THE RIGHT TIME

Excellent batters know that it is all about timing. If a batter swings too early, they will miss the ball. If a batter swings too late, they will miss the ball. Being able to hit a home run means being able to time your swing. You must swing at the right time to ensure that the right part of the bat connects with the ball at the perfect time. Timing is crucial when attempting to hit a home run. Life is no different. Timing is critical when trying to hit a home run in life. The Bible states in Ecclesiastes 3:1 (NKJV), "To everything there is a season. A time for every purpose under heaven." The Bible is clear that timing is everything.

Oftentimes, the difference between success and setback is the time in which action was taken. In all that you seek to do, ask God to help you with the timing. One fact that I can tell you about timing is that when it is the right time, you will definitely know. God has a way of making the right time stand out and feel different than any other time. Remain close to God and know that when it is time to take action, He will ensure that you know.

FOLLOW THROUGH

A batter cannot hit a home run without follow-through. What does that mean? That means committing to a full swing to the point that your arms cross in front of your entire body and the bat goes from one shoulder to the next. There is something that batters do in baseball known as the bunt. A bunt is where the batter turns the bat horizontally and instead of swinging to hit the ball with force, the batter taps the ball for it to roll a short distance. There are logical reasons for a batter to do this, however, none of the reasons include trying to hit a home run. The fact is a home run requires a full swing. Too many of us lack full commitments and follow-through. Instead of going all out and fully committing to something, we will half-commit (half "swing" or "bunt"). You cannot hit a home run if you refuse to be all in. We must follow through. We must finish what we have started. Too many of us have so many unfinished projects. Unfinished home projects. Unfinished work projects. Unfinished personal projects. We will never be able to hit a home run if we do not finish what we have started.

I have discovered that many people love the idea and planning phases of projects. Many people love fantasizing over the full potential of the finished product, however, very few people love the demanding work required between the planning phase and the completion of the product. If you find that the middle phase of a project between conception and completion often proves to be the most difficult phase and far too often ends in you abandoning the work altogether, I want to encourage you with what the Bible affirms in Ecclesiastes 7:8 (NKJV), "The end of a thing is better than its beginning; The patient in spirit is better than the proud in spirit." In other words, if you can somehow gather enough patience to finish what you have started, the end result and fruit of your patience and hard work will produce an indescribable joy and sense of accomplishment on the inside of you that will make it all worth it. The reward will be great both internally and externally. Why? The payoff at the end is always far better than the idea at the beginning. Finish what you started and hit that home run.

A Moment of Reflection
Chapter 3: Life is Like Baseball: How to Hit a Homerun

As you reflect on how "Life is Like Baseball," what are some elements that you absolutely need in order to ensure a successful future?

A Moment of Reflection

A Moment of Reflection

A Moment of Reflection

Chapter 4
LIFE IS LIKE BOXING: HOW TO KNOCK OUT WHAT'S TRYING TO DEFEAT YOU

"I have fought the good fight, I have finished the race, I have kept the faith."
- 2 Timothy 4:7 (New King James Version)

The first six words of this verse confirm the fact that life is not easy. Not only is life not easy, but there are also times when life can be a fight. Jesus warned in John 16:33 that in this life we will have troubles, trials, and even moments of suffering. He also encouraged us by saying in that same verse, "…but be of good cheer, I have overcome the world." There are times when you must fight through trials and certain situations that are weighing very heavily on every aspect of your very being. There are times when you must fight spiritually, emotionally, psychologically, and in some cases physically as to combat the toll that the weight of the fight can place on your physical body. Even though life can be a fight, there are two things that we must always remember. Number one, since Jesus has already overcome every fight that this world has to offer, we will overcome when we include Jesus in our fight. If you do not know what that means, do not worry, this chapter will show you exactly how to include Jesus in your fight. Jesus moves by invitation. He only goes where He is invited. Therefore, if you have not invited Jesus to join you in this fight, then take a moment to do that right now. That invitation is extended through this simple prayer: "Dear Jesus, I recognize you as my Lord and my Savior and I invite you to join me in this fight and in every area of my life. As you join me, lead me. In Jesus' name. Amen."

The second element that we must remember is that there can be no victory without a battle. There can be no testimony without a test. There can be no message without a mess. We all must go through something in order to get to something. There is victory on the other side of whatever battle you are facing. If you hang in there and trust God, you will come out on the other side of this in victory. As the Psalmist David declared in Psalm 30:5b, "Weeping may endure for a night, but joy comes in the morning." Keep your mind stayed on Jesus and stayed on victory, knowing that whatever fight life brings your way, it is only temporary, and everything is going to be ok.

My dad was an avid boxer at one point in his life. He is the reason that I became a fan of boxing at an early age. Saturday mornings were a major bonding time for us because of Saturday morning cable TV boxing. We did not care who was fighting, nor did we care about names or notoriety. We just cared about the fact that they were going to fight. If they were fighting, we were watching.

I will never forget asking my dad one Saturday morning, just as one fight was ending and another was soon to begin, "Dad, what does it take to be a great boxer?" I will never forget that in that moment, as my dad answered my question, God spoke to me at that early age and said, "The same things that your dad is telling you makes a great boxer are the same things that make a great fighter in everyday life. Remember what he is telling you and apply these things to your life." I did exactly that. I made up in my mind that I would take his answer to my question of what makes a great boxer and apply those things to my life. I want to share with you exactly what my dad said to me that day. I pray his answer equips you the way that it equipped me to knock out anything in your life that is trying to defeat you.

My dad, in his wisdom and doing the best that he could to break his answer down into bite-sized pieces so that this 8-year-old could easily understand what was about to be explained, said to me, "Great boxers understand that success in their career can be found in their diligence within three categories. The first category has everything to do with their actions before they get into the ring. The second category has everything to do with their actions once they get into the ring. And the third category has everything to do with their actions while they are in the ring."

Here is the breakdown that my dad gave me. May the following enlighten, encourage, empower, edify, and equip you for the knockout.

BEFORE YOU GET INTO THE RING

Great boxers will tell you that preparation for a fight begins long before the day, week, or month of the actual fight. There is no way you can be ready for a fight, and you have not taken a great deal of time to prepare. The average boxer undergoes intense training for a fight at least a couple of months ahead of the actual fight.

Can you imagine a boxer getting prepared for the very first time on the day of the fight after they step inside of the ring with the other fighter? Imagine the boxer getting into the ring on the day of the fight and for the first time ever starting to do cardio, muscle building, strength, and endurance exercises and training. Everyone would be shocked, appalled, and in fear for the boxer's safety and life. Yet, the truth is, too many of us in life wait until we are already in a fight before we start taking measures that will prepare us for a fight. The best time to train for a fight is when there is no fight. In the boxing world, this is referred to as "conditioning." Conditioning is all about getting you ready for the fight through building strength, endurance, wisdom, and everything else that you need to win before you get into the actual fight.

In life, God has a way of conditioning us that helps prepare us for overcoming whatever fight life may bring our way.

Just like in boxing, the best time to "condition" or "train" for life is when life does not feel like a fight. If we do the proper things prior to certain struggles, we will not be so easily defeated when certain issues arise. For instance, the best time to live on a budget is not when you have financial problems. The time to live on a budget is long before that. The best time to eat healthy is long before you discover that you have health issues. Of course, it is never too late to make changes and you can certainly start new habits at any given time but try not to be the kind of person who buys a fire extinguisher after the house burns down. Think ahead. Plan ahead. Act ahead.

In boxing, effective conditioning requires another person. This person is known as the boxer's trainer. Every great boxer knows the importance of having a great trainer. No boxer can do it all on their own. They not only need the direction, but they need the accountability. The role of the trainer is to help develop habits, thoughts, and behavior in you through discipline and instruction. Their sole job is to help make you better. In everyday life, a trainer would be categorized as a mentor. Just like every boxer must have a trainer designed to make them better, each one of us must have someone in our lives who is designed to make our lives better. Everyone needs a mentor. A great mentor is someone who has been where you are trying to go. Why? You cannot fully lead someone to a place where you have not been. Who do you have in your life that can teach you? Everyone needs to have someone in their life to which they will listen. Everyone needs accountability. To whom do you respect enough to be accountable? Sometimes this person provides direction. At times they may provide feedback or provide accountability. Whatever they are sent by God to provide, the goal is for our lives to improve as a result of having them in it. If you do not have this person in your life, pray about who this can be.

Trainers often function as sparring partners as well. The boxer's sparring partner is the person who gets in the ring with them to work through the strategic plans of attack. Boxers are aware of the fact that their sparring partner is not their enemy. Their sparring partner is their helper. It is simply the person designed to make them superior through challenging them and pushing them to go beyond their comfort zone. God has put a "sparring partner" in all our lives. In life, a good sparring partner challenges you by not just agreeing with everything that you say or do. They assess your theories and methods of doing things. Oftentimes, because sparring partners make us feel uncomfortable, we run or hide from them or even label them as "haters." They are not haters they are helpers. Embrace the questions that challenge you and grow. How can you tell the difference between someone who is genuinely trying to help you and someone who is not? Well, the person who is genuinely trying to help you provides constructive criticism while the person who is not genuinely trying to help you gives destructive criticism. One builds you up and makes you better while the other tears you down and leaves you worse.

Here is a practical example of someone who helps condition you. You borrow money from them, and they want their money back. They are not a hater because they have been asking when you will pay them back. They are someone who just wants you to function in integrity. In addition to that, they are someone that God is using to "train" you on a subconscious level to live in the habit of paying your bills. This person is conditioning you to have a mindset that helps you have and keep good credit.

If you only have friends that agree with everything that you do, you are limiting yourself and hindering your own growth. Growth requires challenge. Good friends challenge us.

Sidenote, do not confuse the word challenge with combat, confront, or confuse. Good friends challenge us in love. It is not hostile nor combative, confrontational, or a cause for confusion.

It is also worth noting that a good sparring partner or trainer pushes you beyond your comfort zone by encouraging you to continue going when you feel like you want to just admit defeat and give up. Great boxers also have the habit of watching videos or previous fights of the opponent they are going to face. By watching the videos, they study and take note of the habits, patterns, and styles of their opponent. In life, it would benefit us to study the habits, patterns, and styles of our spiritual enemy, of the triggers that cause our own unhealthy or negative reactions, and of other people in our lives. Here is a question to help you note those habits, patterns, and styles. What does it look like every time you stress out? In other words, what are the series of events that happen leading up to you becoming stressed out? What are the series of emotions that happen leading up to you becoming stressed out? Feel free to replace "stressed out" with angered, depressed, drinking, smoking, drugs, anxiety, or any number of self-defeating reactions that you may have when life becomes overwhelming or relentless in its fight against you. By asking yourself this question, you gain knowledge of the same patterns and cycles that are used against you. Here is another question. In addition to what happens whenever you react in a negative way, who is involved? Who is the person or who are the people that always seem to be at the root of your negative reactions? Answering these questions will, at the very least, help you grow beyond getting overtaken by the same things. Some people do the same things and get the same negative reactions out of us every single time. At the very least, require a new tactic to get you worked up. I want you to note that I used the words "react" and "reactions." To react to something means to be led in our behavior by a situation or emotion. We want to be careful not to react, but to respond. To respond means to take the time to process and be led in our behavior by wisdom and strategic thinking. A reaction is impulsive while a response often takes time. Always seek to overcome the temptation of reacting and become a person who has the healthy and productive habit of responding.

Great boxers know the importance of a healthy diet. They know how important it is to monitor what they deposit into their body. In life, it is important that we monitor what we place into our body. This pertains to more than what we deposit into our body physically. This also pertains to what we put into our body mentally, emotionally, and psychologically. We do this by guarding the people that we intermingle with, the conversations that we have, the shows that we watch, and the music that we listen to. There is no way that we can live a fully disciplined life without having fully disciplined habits. There is no way that we can have fully disciplined habits and be open to going everywhere, watching everything, and listening to anything. Boundaries and discipline are necessary for a healthy and effective life. Why? Everything plants a seed and certain fruit I do not want to harvest and release from my body.

ONCE YOU GET INTO THE RING

Just like discipline is key for a boxer prior to getting into the ring, it is also key to the effectiveness of the boxer once inside of the ring. Boxers cannot get inside of the ring and just start wildly swinging and flailing their arms all over the place simply because they are determined to win. An undisciplined boxer usually gets knocked out. Frustration, anger, hurt, and wounds cannot force us into a lack of discipline. A skilled boxer remains disciplined regardless of their condition or the status of the fight. In life, we must remain the most disciplined when we are in the toughest fight of our lives. The spiritual enemy is unfair.

People are unfair. Life is unfair. People can be malicious and spreading all sorts of hurt and evil. Life can be overwhelming, however, regardless of how unfair things and people are, always remain disciplined. A disciplined boxer is a victorious boxer. A disciplined person is a victorious person. The Bible has much to say about living a disciplined life. One of the most impactful scriptures related to discipline is found in 2 Timothy 1:7, "For God has not given us a spirit of fear, but of power and of love and of a sound mind." The word "sound" translated means "disciplined." This scripture is letting us know that God has already given us a disciplined mind. With that being said, it is up to us to hold onto what we have already been given. If I were to give you the literal and practical translation of 2 Timothy 1:7, it would read like this: "God has not given us a fear-based mindset that is timid, cowardly, or powerless. God has given us power and ability to love and be disciplined in our minds during tough times." Discipline will guide you into your destiny.

Once in the ring, every boxer must have a mouthpiece. The mouthpiece helps protect the boxer's teeth and surrounding soft tissue. The mouthpiece also helps guard against jaw fractures and protects the boxer's mouth from other possible long-term damage. The mouthpiece is necessary. The boxer must do something to guard their mouth. In life, we must have a mouthpiece; not a physical mouthpiece, but something in place to help guard our mouths. Like every child has heard at some point "watch your mouth," guard the words that are coming out of your mouth. Do not just say whatever you want, simply because you are feeling it. Remember what I mentioned earlier regarding reacting versus responding. Do not allow frustration, hurt, pain, anger, bitterness, anxiety, fear, or any other negative emotion to cause you to become undisciplined in your speech. You must make up in your mind that no matter what life throws your way, you are going to guard your mouth. The Bible has much to say about the power of our words. Proverbs 18:21a states, "Death and life are in the power of the tongue… " Ephesians 4:29 declares, "Let no corrupt word proceed out of your mouth, but what is good for necessary edification, that it may impart grace to the hearers." James Chapter 3 speaks a great deal about the power of our tongue. In fact, we learn in James Chapter 3 that our mouths have the power to direct, destroy, and delight. Our words can produce some incredibly beautiful elements and some very tragic elements. We carry the power in our mouths to speak components of our lives into existence. That is why I always tell people, "If you do not like what you see, watch what you say." Many of us have spoken problems into our lives. Many of us have declared hardship and negativity for years and now we are fighting to overcome it. Overcoming begins with canceling the confession of it. Stop calling your spouse crazy. You are declaring crazy over their life. Speak positively and initiate change in the atmosphere with your words. You can speak your reality.

WHILE YOU ARE IN THE RING BE QUICK

Skilled boxers move quickly. They do not prolong action. Keep in mind that once they are in the fight, they have already planned and strategized long before the current moment. Therefore, there is no reason to delay action. Once, you have planned your work, do not delay action in working your plan. Strategize, then implement. Be quick to correct actions. Be quick to change directions. Be quick to revise and restart when things are not going well or as planned. In an even more practical sense, be quick to forgive. Be quick to do what you can to restore relationships. Be quick to solve any issues or outstanding problems that you may be facing. Once you know what to do, do it.

BE ACCURATE

Trained boxers are accurate. How is accuracy judged? Well, boxers know that their punches are accurate when they connect. They know that there has been an accurate connection when their opponent is affected in some sense by it. Make moves that positively affect your negative situation. Make moves that bring healing. Make moves that bring peace. Make moves that bring hope. Make financial moves that raise your credit score, add to your savings, or keep you from building new debt. Make relationship moves that decrease stress and raise peace and love. Great boxers are not concerned about one big knockout punch as much as they are concerned about wearing their opponent down one punch at a time. In time, the big punch will come, but it often comes after a series of consistent and accurate punches. Do not overwhelm yourself by trying to solve everything right now. Be concerned about "wearing it down" with consistent and accurate moves. Instead of overwhelming yourself with all the financial debt that you have, focus on one item that you can pay down until you pay it off. Once, you pay off that item, shift your attention to the next item. Certainly, you continue to pay all your bills, however, you focus on one by paying extra until it is completely paid off. The key is to do something. Small steps lead to big advancements.

BE POWERFUL

Power changes an atmosphere. A great boxer knows that while you must be quick and accurate, you must also have a power-packed punch. Boxers use several exercises that help them build their power through consistently working on their technique and growth. The best way to have a power-packed punch in your everyday life is through fellowship, faith, and focus. You build your power through consistent fellowship with God. Consistent fellowship with God is maintained through prayer. As I stated in Chapter 1: Life is Like Football, prayer is simply a conversation with God. God is always open and available to have a conversation with you. God is not looking for you to be deep in your conversation with Him. He is simply looking for you to be YOU. God loves authenticity. He loves genuine prayers from the heart. You will discover that the more you pray, the more your prayers develop. Much like a child learning to speak continues to evolve in their vocabulary, the same happens in your prayer life when you are consistent. Having fellowship with God will help you grow and develop in your faith in God. Being that you will begin to see your life change for the better because of your prayer time with God, it will become easier to trust Him even in moments when you cannot necessarily trace Him. At its core, faith is acting like God told the truth. What truth? The truths that we read about in the Bible. As you read the Bible, begin to take ownership of those stories of victory by incorporating them into your conversations with God and your personal declarations over your life. As you read a story such as David and Goliath, begin to thank God that He is also helping you destroy the giants in your life. Begin to declare aloud that every giant in your life is being destroyed through the power of God working in you and through you. As you begin to stand on God's Word, you will discover that He always stands by His Word. In addition to fellowship and faith, power is built through focus. What you focus on is what dominates your life. If you focus on obstacles, obstacles will dominate your life. However, if you focus on solutions, solutions will dominate your life. If you focus on your past, your past will dominate your life. However, if you focus on building a successful bridge from your present into your future, then this hope of what lies ahead will dominate your life. If you desire more power in your life, emotionally, spiritually, mentally, or even physically, you must commit to a life of consistent fellowship with God, faith in God, and focus on the positive and productive things of your present that lead you to a desired future.

BE DEFENSIVE

An incredible boxer knows that while they must throw punches, they must also guard against punches. Boxing is all about having both a solid offense and defense.

While attacking offensively, skilled boxers recognize the importance of staying on guard. Boxers must protect themselves. What does that mean for us in everyday life? We must have boundaries in place that keep us from getting knocked down by the very things we are trying to overcome. God has boundaries.

The story of Adam and Eve in the garden of Eden where God told them not to touch a certain tree is really a story about boundaries. If God had boundaries, then you know we must have boundaries. It is necessary that we be intentional about putting things in place that help keep us moving forward. Let us use finances again as an example. I often use finances as an example because it seems to be an area people struggle with the most. As a sidenote, do you know that the Bible talks more about money than anything else? People struggled with finances then like many of us struggle with them now. If you are focusing on getting out of debt and building excellent credit, you must create certain disciplines and put certain items in place that keep you from frivolously spending money and deepening the hole that you are trying to climb out of. Decide that you do not need to rush to every sale that you see advertised on television. You do not have to dine out every weekend. In fact, make participating in a good sale, or dining out on the weekend a reward for a goal accomplished and not a habit that created the financial problem to begin with. As you continue to move forward offensively, always make sure you are moving forward defensively as well.

BE DISCIPLINED

This concept is worth repeating because exceptional boxers know that the same discipline that is required before you get into the ring, and once you get into the ring, is also required after you get into the ring. Discipline wins from the beginning to the end. Boxers cannot afford to lose their discipline while in the fight. Discipline is the ability to control yourself and work consistently hard in a particular way without the need for supervision. Discipline starts in the mind. It is a mindset. My external behavior and actions are disciplined because of the battles that I have won in my mind. Considering I have overcome temptations to do counterproductive things in my mind, my external actions simply align themselves with that internal decision. Just like a boxer tries to break the discipline of their opponent, you will discover that certain things arise daily that are designed to break your discipline. Be determined to stay disciplined regardless of what issues arise in your life.

BE COURAGEOUS

Just like discipline wins fights, courage wins fights as well. Every punch that is thrown in a fight has the potential to break down a boxer's courage. At the end of the day, who likes to get punched? No one I know. However, boxers know that punches come with the territory. Boxers enter fights knowing that punches will be thrown in their direction. Despite that, they also enter the fight having decided that they will not let any of the punches, regardless of their intensity, affect their courage. We must have the same mindset. Life has a way of throwing punches. We must expect it because life is just life. Again, Jesus made it clear that this life would not be easy. We expect punches to be thrown in our direction, however, we must conclude that these punches, regardless of intensity will not affect our courage. In all things, remain courageous. You can do this. In fact, you have been doing this. You have already overcome so much that was designed to destroy you. Take a moment and look back over the tough times of your life. You have truly survived and overcome a lot. In fact, I guarantee that you have experienced so much success and victory in your life, that you have forgotten some of the things that you have overcome. You have come too far to let these current punches affect your confidence. God did not bring you this far just to bring you this far. Whatever you do, do not judge your entire "life's book" by the chapter you are currently on. Determine to remain confident and watch life continue to improve, even if it is one small step at a time. Be courageous and remain courageous.

BE INTELLIGENT

Experienced boxers are intelligent boxers. Sometimes being intelligent means being able to adjust. I created a personal proverb for my life that says, "Blessed are the flexible for they shall never be broken." The greater your ability to adjust, the greater your chances are for victory. Being an intelligent boxer also means being able to think ahead. Accomplished boxers must have a certain level of foresight. They must be able to have some ability to see what may happen before it happens. That is what wisdom is. Wisdom is the ability to see the future consequences of your present actions. Just because something worked before does not mean it will work this time. Sometimes we can get so caught up on what God told us that we cannot hear what He is telling us. Great boxers know that every opponent is different. Therefore, they cannot approach every opponent the same way. The strategy that was used to defeat the last opponent could very well be stopped with this one. They must structure their approach based on their knowledge of the current opponent. That is how intelligence works in our everyday life. Living life with intelligence means living life with wisdom. It means being able to make the necessary adjustments based on our knowledge of the current situation. Your strategies vary as your goals remain the same.

One final note regarding intelligence is that great boxers know their own strengths, limitations, and weaknesses. We must be so rooted in reality that we are very aware of our own strengths, limitations, and weaknesses. Let me also add the word "triggers" to that list. Know what triggers you. Intelligence helps you live a life that is so aware of these things that you create a plan with them in mind.

So, there you have it. This is exactly what my dad told me the day I asked him about what makes a great boxer. All these tools are not just for professional boxers, but they are for professional goal setters and life conquerors like you and I. Use them and knock out everything that is trying to defeat you.

A Moment of Reflection
Chapter 4: Life is Like Boxing: How to Knock Out What's Trying to Defeat You

As you reflect on how "Life is Like Boxing," what can you proactively implement in your life right now that will prove to be beneficial for you as you journey forward in life?

A Moment of Reflection

A Moment of Reflection

A Moment of Reflection

Chapter 5
LIFE IS LIKE GOLF: HOW TO REACH YOUR GOALS

"But as for you, be strong and do not give up, for your work will be rewarded."
- 2 Chronicles 15:7b (NIV)
"May he give you the desire of your heart and make all your plans succeed."
- Psalm 20:4 (NIV)
"Commit to the Lord whatever you do, and he will establish your plans."
- Proverbs 16:3 (NIV)

I will never forget my first day out on the golf course. It was terrible and not something I should even be sharing right here. I mean, it was beyond embarrassing. It was so bad that the group I was with thought I was trying to hustle them. Now you know that's awful when people think there is no way you play like that. Ok, let me explain what happened.

I met my wife in early 2000. She was and continues to be everything I could ever want in a wife and mother of my children. I was completely smitten. I mean, instantly in love. Well, because I was raised right by my mom and dad, I was taught that you do not start officially dating a young lady until you ask her father for permission. This is one tradition that many young people have escaped we need to return to if the possibility exists. At any rate, I found out that her father loved to golf. Growing up playing miniature golf, I thought, "How hard could this be? I mean, isn't regular golf just like miniature golf except without the robotic animals, small windmills blocking the holes and tunnels to the holes, and pretty lights and statues? I mean other than those things, isn't it the same thing?" For anyone wondering, the answer is a mega NO! They are nothing close to the same thing. They are drastically different. In my ignorance, I approached my now father-in-law, but then father of the young lady I was hoping to date then marry, and I told him that I needed to talk to him about something. Without missing a beat, he said to me, "Do you golf?" Again, in my ignorance, without missing a beat, I replied, "Of course I do." He said, "Great, let's go Sunday after church." You should have seen me trying to maintain a certain level of confidence and hope all week by repeating the phrase, "You can do this, it's just like miniature golf, but without the Christmas parade-like atmosphere." Sidenote, it is possible to continuously repeat the wrong phrases to yourself repeatedly and build a very misinformed confidence. Trust me, I know from experience.

The big day arrives and here we are out on the golf course. I will never forget. It was me, my father-in-law, my wife's brother (who actually ended up marrying my sister, which is another subject for another book), and one of my father-in-law's good friends. All these guys were great golfers. I was the only one who never stepped foot on an actual golf course before, and it showed, tremendously. My first hole I actually parred. In golf, to par means to make it into the hole in the actual predetermined number of strokes that a proficient golfer should require. God felt so sorry for me in that moment, that He helped me supernaturally par my first hole. Well, I am not sure if I did something to upset God after that or not because there was no supernatural assistance after that first hole. It deteriorated in record-breaking time. Somehow, I perfected the art of hitting the ball where no ball has ever gone before. It was sad. So sad that at one point, my father in law's friend said those infamous words that I mentioned in the beginning, "Oh you're not fooling me, you're trying to hustle us." He then turned to the other guys and said, "He's trying to hustle us." We were not playing for anything, and additionally, the game was halfway over. No one runs a hustle in golf for this long. That day ended so poorly that my father-in-law turned to me at the end and said, "Any guy who would take the time to come out here and talk to me about dating my daughter and have no clue how to golf, has my blessing." Whew! I did it. I got his blessing. I mean it came with embarrassment and a few awkward silent moments along the way, but I left with his blessing.

Several years later, I decided that my body no longer wanted to participate in pick-up games of football and did not seem overly excited about the basketball pick-up games either. I decided that I really needed and wanted to pursue golf. I am very much still in the beginning stages but at least I know that it is nothing like miniature golf.

As I pursued my interest in the game of golf, I called my father-in-law one day and asked him to help me learn the game.

My father-in-law and I first went to shop for my very own golf clubs. As we shopped for golf clubs, he strongly recommended that I get fitted golf clubs. Fitted golf clubs are clubs that are specifically designed for my hands. They are tailor-made for me, and I discovered that having clubs that are designed specifically for you greatly improves your game. It is important that we pursue the goals and dreams that God has designed specifically for us. There is a calling, purpose, plan, and destiny with your name on it.

God created it with you on His mind. I encourage you not to do anything until you know exactly what God wants you to do. The Bible states in Proverbs 3:5-6, "Trust in the Lord with all your heart, and lean not on your own understanding. In all your ways acknowledge Him, and He shall direct your paths."

Now that I had my own golf clubs, it was time to learn some particularly important golf game tips. My father-in-law immediately gave me ten tips that not only instantly improved my game, and I say that very loosely, but it improved my focus and success in life. I am going to share with you the ten tips that he shared with me and pray that it helps you the way it continues to help me.

VISUALIZE IT

He reminded me of how he does not do anything without seeing what needs to be done. I remembered how I watched him approach the ball, look off in the distance toward the hole, look down at the ball, kneel down and really consider what needed to be done to effectively advance the ball. In essence, he was seeing it done before it was getting done. I often tell people, you must learn how to see it before you see it, meaning, see it in your mind. Perhaps see it spiritually. See it in faith. See it already being done before it gets done. You will never accomplish anything that you cannot see. See yourself launching that business. See yourself obtaining your degree. See yourself buying that house. See yourself getting married. See yourself having children. Whatever the goal may be, see it in your mind and spirit before you see it in the natural.

CHECK YOUR ALIGNMENT

My father-in-law taught me the importance of lining up the lines on the golf club to the ball. He also taught me the importance of aligning my shoulders, hips, and feet so that I can truly maximize my swing. The most effective swing is one that is set up by great alignment. In life, we must always do an alignment check. Who are you aligned with? Who are your friends? Who are the people you consider to be your inner circle? I can discern much about a person based on the people they align themselves with. Before you align yourself with anyone, be sure to check out who they align themselves with. In addition to who you align yourself with, it is important to know what you align yourself with. What are your values? What are your priorities? Again, you can determine much about a person by what they align themselves with. Just like a car needs a wheel alignment after a certain amount of time, all of us could stand to check our life alignment after a certain amount of time. You would be surprised how quickly your circle and priorities can change if you are not deliberate about how you align yourself.

PRACTICE PATIENCE

Golf is most certainly not a game for impatient people. If you lack patience, golf will only frustrate you. Golf is all about taking your time and performing the right action, the right way. Performing the right action, the right way is not something that can be rushed. More so, it is not something that should be rushed. To consistently perform the right action, the right way, you must take time to consider the right and best approach. Golf is a game of constant evaluation. You are constantly evaluating which golf club to use and exactly how to use it. You are constantly evaluating distance. You are constantly evaluating the wind and weather. You are constantly evaluating angles. There are so many aspects to evaluate, and it is impossible to accurately do so without patience. Life is the same way. Life requires patience. Effective decisions take time. Reaching goals take time. Strategizing takes time. If it is worth having, it is worth working for, and the work needed is not a quick work. It is a work that involves patience. Learn to slow down and evaluate as you pursue your goals. Be patient with yourself. You may not get it right the first time. It may not happen overnight. It may not happen in the period that you desire for it to happen. It may not happen in the manner that you desire for it to happen. It may require strategizing repeatedly. It may require making some mistakes. Mistakes are just missed takes. Get up and take it again. There may be times of frustration or weariness but keep working towards that goal. Anything worth possessing is worth your patience.

DEVELOP LONG-TERM AND SHORT-TERM GOALS

In golf, sometimes the hole is far away and sometimes the hole is remarkably close. While there is a such thing as a hole in one, those occurrences are rare. My father-in-law has hit a hole in one before, but again, that is incredibly rare. Golfers do not approach the start of the hole that they are pursuing, thinking that they must get a hole in one. They approach the start of that hole contemplating what they need to do to not only get the ball in a much better position but get the ball in the absolute best position possible for the goal of getting the ball into the hole. As they consider and strategize their plan of attack, they are setting long-term goals; long-term because the hole is far away and long-term because it will require more than a single hit. It will require a hit that is the perfect set-up for the next hit. See, golfers are always thinking about the best action to take now so that the next move is even easier. That is exactly what long-term planning in life is about. It is all about deciding on the absolute best move to make now so that your next move is even easier. Every move you make in life should be the perfect set-up for the next move that you are going to make in life. All your moves in life should complement each other. They should all have relationship. Your ultimate goal should be seen in every move that you make in life. Every move you make in your advancement toward your long-term goal should be considered as a short-term goal. In other words, the golfer's short-term goal is to get the ball closer to the hole by hitting it to a certain location. Your short-term goal in life should be a step toward your long-term goal. All your short-term goals should land you at the door of your long-term goal. For instance, if my long-term goal is to start a business, my short-term goal should be to find a mentor who has displayed success in starting a business. I will talk more about this momentarily. In the meantime, list your long-term goal and all the short-term goals required to achieve that long term goal.

BE AWARE OF THE TRAPS

Golfers know to be on the lookout for the sand traps and the water hazards. Being that they know these traps and hazards exist, they do everything necessary and humanly possible to avoid hitting their ball into one of these traps. Now because no one is perfect, sometimes golfers do hit their ball into one of these traps or hazards, but they do not stay there. They get their ball out of there as quickly as possible. If it lands in the water, they may just have to count the loss and move on. In life, we must be aware of the potential traps and hazards that lie in our path. Your spiritual enemy does not want you to be happy or successful, therefore, he will go out of his way to set traps and hazards designed to delay or distract you from reaching your goal, or perhaps prevent you from reaching your goal altogether. Whatever you do, live with your eyes and ears open, being on the lookout for traps and hazards that come in many forms. Be vigilant. Make deliberate and purpose- driven moves while remaining alert and aware of everything around you. A great rule to live by is whatever does not help me, hurts me, period. Keep that in mind and you will become a professional at instantly categorizing things and people while avoiding potential traps and hazards. Things and people are either for you or against you and in the words of my grandmother as she concluded the church announcements every Sunday, "Govern yourself accordingly."

DEVELOP A ROUTINE

Every golfer has a routine. Have you ever seen a golfer approach the ball, kneel down, stare off into the distance, stand back up straight, back away from the ball, do several practice swings, approach the ball again, do some half swings, then finally hit the ball? Do you know what you just witnessed? You just witnessed that golfer's routine. Routines vary. Golfers adopt the routine that is best for them. They adopt the routine that brings out their best game. In life, we must establish the best routine that helps us maximize life. The ideal routine for your life, places you in the best mental, emotional, spiritual, and physical space possible. The best routine optimizes every area of your life. If you are not experiencing the success that you would like to experience, I can guarantee that the problem lies within your daily routine. Evaluate your current routine and ask yourself is it positioning you for optimal results. If not, do not adjust your goal, adjust your routine. You do not get what you want out of life, you get what you put into life. Your routine will reveal to you exactly what you are putting into life.

IDENTIFY YOUR WEAKNESS

Every golfer has a weakness, but do you know what they do? They deal with it. They work to make that weakness a strength. Understand, that you will never fix what you refuse to face. Face it and faith it. Face it by tackling your weakness head on and do everything within your power to turn that weakness into a strength. When you do what you can, God will do what you cannot. That truth right there is what we hang on to as we faith it. To faith it means, as I work on my weakness, I take comfort and hope in the fact that this will not always be a weakness because I am not working on it alone. I am working on it with God. As I am doing what I can, God is doing what I cannot. I am working on my weakness while seeing myself in the future where this weakness is no longer a weakness. Do not run from your weaknesses. We all have them. Face them, fight them, and overcome them. Philippians 4:13 declares, "I can do all things through Christ who strengthens me." With God you can and with God you will. With consistent effort and focus you can diminish your weakness and find ultimate victory over it.

VISIT THE RANGE REGULARLY

My father-in-law told me that I needed to visit the driving range or golf course at least twice a week. He said the best way to improve my game is to practice my game, and the best way to practice my game is to show up to the range. If you are going to hit your goals, then you need to build in regular visits to whatever helps you accomplish that goal. This may not mean physically showing up somewhere, but it does mean connecting on some level. This could mean "visiting" helpful resources online on a regular basis. Perhaps it means reading a book. You must determine what your "visit" and "range or course" looks like. Visiting your range or course twice a week may mean setting aside time to conduct extensive research on a specific topic associated with your ultimate goal. Perhaps it means setting aside time to sit with your mentor, either online, on the phone, or in person. Once you determine what your visits and range or course look like, be consistent in doing it at least twice a week. Imagine the progress you could make through simply being consistent in "visiting your range or course" at least twice a week. If you want to open a restaurant, imagine the progress you could make if you connected with something or someone twice a week either online or in person as it relates to the restaurant business. There is much success connected to simply being consistent in showing up. Show up regularly and watch the progress you make toward accomplishing your eventual goal.

PLAY WITH PLAYERS BETTER THAN YOU

Golfers know that if they want to improve their golf game, they need to surround themselves with people who are better than them. You do not ever want to be the strongest or best person in your circle. Why? If you are the strongest, who do you look to for motivation? Where do you go from there? If you are not the strongest, you always have motivation right in front of you. You always have a goal to hit. You always have something to strive for. The best motivation is the tangible one that is right in front of you. Some people have a need to be the strongest because it feeds their ego. However, wise people desire to have someone stronger than them surrounding them because it feeds their goal. The confident person is grateful to be around the person who is stronger than them. They enjoy having that person motivate them and create momentum in them. The insecure person misses the blessing, beauty, and benefit of having someone stronger than them around because oftentimes they are living life in light of their perceived shortcomings instead of living life through their God-given potentials. Stronger people encircling us is golden. Take full advantage of that blessing and enhance your life as a result. If you fully embrace all that can be gained from having someone stronger than you in your circle, you will discover that your life is improving every day.

LOVE THE GAME

Great golfers love the game of golf. It is their love for the game that serves as constant motivation to work on their game. Their love for the game keeps them striving for better and keeps them showing up with excitement. Their love for golfing brings success. You will never reach your full potential or your greatest level of success doing something that you do not love. If you want to experience success, start with doing something that you love. The worst kind of employee is the one who dislikes their job. They never give it their all. In fact, they often give the bare minimum. They often give just enough to get by. The best employee is the one who loves their job. They are often going far, over, above, and beyond the call of duty. They do not mind showing up early and staying late. Their mindset and entire approach to the job is different from the one who despises their job. Always do what you love. If you love it, then you will survive the disappointments and setbacks. If you love it, then you will always give it your all. You will always strive for better. You will always work toward something greater than the current situation. Your entire heart and effort go into what you love. If you are doing something right now that you do not love, start making the necessary moves to transition towards doing something that you do love. Life is too short to spend time doing something that we do not love. Successful people do what they love. Find what you love and find success. You will always hit your goal when your goal is connected to what you love.

The day my father-in-law and I had this conversation was the day my life progressed. It has continued progressing ever since. I pray that today, in this moment, your life progresses and continues to grow and improve because of these ten golf tips. It is amazing to me how much life is just like golf.

A Moment of Reflection
Chapter 5: Life is Like Golf: How to Reach Your Goals

As you reflect on how "Life is Like Golf," what are your ultimate life goals and what steps have you taken, or can you take today that will bring those goals even closer to becoming a reality?

A Moment of Reflection

A Moment of Reflection

A Moment of Reflection

Chapter 6
LIFE IS LIKE SOCCER: HOW TO BUILD THE PERFECT TEAM

"But select capable men from all the people—men who fear God, trustworthy men who hate dishonest gain—and appoint them as officials over thousands, hundreds, fifties and tens." - Exodus 18:21 (NIV)
"Then the Lord said to Gideon, "By the three hundred men who lapped I will save you and deliver the Midianites into your hand. Let all the other people go, every man to his place." - Judges 7:7 (NKJV)

In 2002, American clergyman and renown leadership trainer, John C. Maxwell, authored a book entitled, Teamwork Makes the Dream Work. This book title turned into a phrase that quickly caught on and continues to get emphasized today more than ever before. There is such profound truth in this one statement. While many people pride themselves on working alone, God never intended for any of us to work alone. I am certain you have heard people say, oftentimes out of frustration, "I don't need anyone." Well, while that can sound like a statement of independence and strength, the truth is, we do need people. We are all pieces of God's puzzle, and our work is incomplete if we refuse to work together. Jesus never sent people out alone. He always sent people out in groups. Oftentimes, Jesus would retreat with his disciples, Peter, James, and John. God's goal is for us to find the other pieces of the puzzle that He has created for us to work with as a team. While individuals win trophies, teams win championships. Much of your success in life hinges on your ability to find your team. If you can get the right team around you, you will truly be unstoppable.

In Exodus 18, Moses' father-in-law went to visit him and was deeply disturbed by what he saw Moses doing. Thousands upon thousands of people approached him daily for a variety of reasons. They all looked to Moses as their sole provider and answer for every kind of issue they could experience. Moses' father-in-law said, and I paraphrase, "What is going on here? "Moses said, and again, I paraphrase, "Well, the people come to me every day for different things, and I help them with whatever they need." Moses' father-in-law said, "Man this does not make any sense. You are so far in over your head. There is no way you can continue to operate like this. You need to get a team of people around you who can help you manage all of this. A team will make all this better for everyone. Starting with you!"

In Judges 7, God told Gideon that He was going to put the perfect team around him for the battle into which he was heading. Gideon started out with over 30,000 people. While this may sound like a lot of people, the army that Gideon was going to fight had 132,000. Talk about being outnumbered! As if that is not scary enough, God then told Gideon that he had too many people on his team. Wait, 30,000 versus 132,000 sounds to me like Gideon did not have quite enough people on his team. However, God's ways are not our ways, and His thoughts are not our thoughts. Often, His plans seem to go against everything we would think to do. Being the obedient person that he was, Gideon decided to allow God to make the necessary cuts on the team. I can tell you for a fact, that God would have grown weary of me asking repeatedly, "God, are you sure we are not doing this backwards? I mean, they have 132,000 while I have 30,000. Did you mean to tell me that I need to host an open call and get some more soldiers in here?" God knew exactly what He was doing. God took Gideon's army from over 30,000 down to 300. There are several lessons here, but the two that stand out the most are the facts that you can have too many people on your team and with the right team, you can overcome anything. The game of soccer provides great insight on how to build the perfect team. I want to give you eight elements that I learned from watching different soccer teams. These eight elements will most certainly help you build your perfect team; a team that can accomplish anything.

Before we break down the elements on how to build an effective team, it is important to know that the game of soccer absolutely cannot be played without a goal. What is soccer without a goal? It is just running around with a ball. Such is the same in everyday life. What is life without a goal? It is just running around without purpose. Life without a goal is a life of frivolous habits. We cannot effectively navigate through this life if we do not have a goal. It is worth asking yourself every now and then what your goal is. It is also worth reviewing your goal from time to time. Complaining and displaying frustration do not produce positive change, but goals do. Produce a goal. If you do not know where you are headed, then you will stay where you are.

The Bible admonishes us in Habakkuk 2:2 to "Write the vision and make it plain." Statistically speaking, when you write down your vision, you have a 90% greater chance of accomplishing it. So, write it down.

In a soccer game, you will always see someone blocking the goal and ensuring that the opposing team never scores. This is expected. It is part of the game. Knowing that someone is positioned to stop them from scoring does not stop the other team from trying. They pursue the goal even with someone standing in front of it. Life is the same way. Nothing comes easy. People and circumstances will often try to stand between us and our goal. However, do not let that discourage you or prevent you from pursuing your goal anyway. Despite someone standing in front of the goal, soccer teams still score. You must decide that despite situations, or people standing in your way, you will still hit your goal. Soccer teams know that with teamwork, they can get past whoever or whatever is blocking the goal. You must have the same mindset. With teamwork, you can get past whoever or whatever is blocking your goal. With that being said, let us talk about how to build this team.

KNOW HOW MANY PEOPLE YOU NEED

Both Moses and Gideon had to decide how many people they needed on their team. In fact, every time you see teams being built throughout the Bible, there was a decision that had to be made regarding how many people. Even if the Bible does not mention that specific conversation, just know that it was always a consideration. The game of soccer is no different. In fact, every sport must make this decision. How many people do they need?

Did you know that there are actually a few varying types of soccer. I discovered that there is traditional outdoor soccer, indoor soccer, beach soccer, street soccer, freestyle soccer, and futsal. The number of people needed depends on which type of soccer you are playing. For instance, traditional outdoor soccer has eleven people per team on the field at a time. However, beach soccer typically has five people per team playing at a time.

Life is no different. The number of people needed for your team depends on what you are doing, what you are trying to accomplish, and what your plan is to get there. First, you must decide on your goal. From there you must decide on your strategy to reach your goal. Then, from there, you determine exactly how many people are needed to work the strategy that leads you to your goal. Always remember that you need someone but may not need everyone.

EVERYONE NEEDS TO HAVE THE SAME FOCUS

Every member of the soccer team must be focused on the same component, the goal. While their roles within the goal varies, their focus and mindset must be the same. No soccer team can be successful if everyone is trying to do their own thing. If they are all running in different directions, trying to accomplish different personal goals, they will not win. Life works the same way. Everyone on your team must have the same focus. There must be a common goal. Like soccer, everyone on your team has a different position to play, but it is all based on the common goal. If the people on your team are moving in different directions trying to accomplish personal goals, your team will not hit your ultimate goal. Ensure the people on your team want what you want. Effective teams move in the same direction.

EVALUATE YOUR SKILLSET

Soccer teams must know exactly who and what they have on their team. They must know the strengths and weaknesses of every player on the team. No player is an expert at everything. However, every player is an expert at something. Therefore, the idea is to fuse everyone's strengths together as they work toward the common goal. Each player's strength should perfectly complement the other players and team as a whole. When strengths are perfectly aligned, weaknesses diminish in power and influence. In fact, weaknesses can be worked on without being a hindering factor when strengths are perfectly aligned and correctly utilized. Just like a soccer team must evaluate and know the strengths of the players on the team, you must also evaluate and know the strengths of the players on your team. You must know who can do what? The answer to this question is not based on who you like the most or to whom you are the closest. The answer to this question is solely based on your personal knowledge of an individual's skillset. Knowing who can do what, helps you correctly position the people on your team. Who is a great communicator? Who is a great writer? Who is the most resourceful? Who is the most consistent? Who is the most stable financially, emotionally, spiritually, and physically? Who is the most educated, experienced, or knowledgeable in this particular area? The list can be as extensive as you need it to be. Continue to evaluate and ask questions until you have properly structured your all-star team. It is also extremely healthy and beneficial to evaluate your own skillset. In what areas do you thrive and soar? In what areas do you really need help? Understand that successful people are not people who have all the answers or know how to do it all. Successful people are people who know how to surround themselves with people who are strong where they are weak. They know how to surround themselves with people who have the answers they do not have and can do the things that they cannot do. Remember, we were created to work in teams, not in isolation.

FILL THE GAPS

Frequently, soccer players go on attack. That means that they begin to move away from their assigned area and pursue (or attack) the goal. When that happens, there is a gap left where that player was before leaving it to attack the goal. When that player leaves, another player must quickly make the transition to fill in the gap. There are times in life where your time and attention may get pulled away from a particular item, project, or area you were working on. When that happens, you need someone on your team who can fill in the gap that your absence leaves behind. Many times, when neighbors leave town, another neighbor will make sure that the trash cans are still pulled out on garbage service day or perhaps any packages left on the porch are collected. This is an example of having someone on your team who can fill in the gaps. Ask yourself, who do you have around you that can fill in the gaps for you should your time and attention be needed elsewhere. This is not a person who does your job. This is simply the person who can keep your job active until you return.

AWARENESS IS A MUST

There are so many moving parts on the field during a soccer game. As a result, everyone on the team must remain aware of what is always going on. Players cannot allow distractions, particularly from people in the stands, to take their mind off what they are doing or needing to do. There is much activity occurring in the soccer arena that is not beneficial to the players on the field. Players must learn to ignore anything or anyone that is not helping them be a productive team member in the game. Often, games are won or lost based on how players managed distractions. All players must keep their head in the game. Life works the same way. Individuals on your team must remain aware of what is always happening. Distractions can prevent you from reaching your goal if they dominate your time and attention. Players on your team cannot be distracted players. They must be very present emotionally, spiritually, mentally, and many times physically. Just like the players on a soccer team, all the players on your team must keep their head in the game. Distracted players can destroy your progress if the distraction is not addressed and overcome.

Awareness means exhibiting discernment. Discernment is the ability to see beneath what is being shown on the surface. A person with discernment can sense the true motives and intentions in someone's heart that reside beneath the words that are coming out of their mouth. A person with discernment can hear all the right words coming out of someone's mouth and still notice evil or negative motives. Great team players remain aware through being free from distractions and filled with discernment.

WORK HARD EVEN WHEN IT IS NOT YOUR TURN

As a soccer game is being played, only one person can have the ball at a time. However, the other players cannot afford to slow down, relax, or take a break simply because they do not have the ball. What they do when they do not have the ball is just as important, and oftentimes more important, as what they do when they do have the ball. I believe you can really see the integrity and commitment of a teammate when they do not have the ball. Next time you watch a soccer game, watch away from the ball. Take note of what the players are doing when they do not have the ball. In fact, take note of what the players are doing when the ball is not in their area at all. In life, it matters what people do when they do not have the ball. In other words, it matters what people do when it is not their turn. It matters what people do when it is not their time to shine. It matters what people do when the spotlight is not on them. Unfortunately, there are too many people who are not concerned about anything or anyone outside of themselves. There are several people who lie dormant until it is their turn. They are completely checked out, disconnected, and uninterested until their name is called. Suddenly, when it is their turn, they come alive and are full of excitement. Pay attention to those types of people. They are not solid team members. You need people on your team who work just as hard for others as they do for themselves. Whether it is for them, someone else, or the team in general, you need someone who gives 100 percent every single time. People who give 100 percent every time have a clear understanding that it is not about them, but it is about the team as a whole and reaching the goal that the team is striving to reach.

IF YOU FALL DOWN, DO NOT STAY DOWN

Soccer is a very fast-paced game. Players are constantly running and shifting all over the field. Being that there is so much movement and players are constantly running, you often see players fall. In fact, given the nature of the game, falling is expected, but please note that whenever players fall, they do not stay down. They immediately pop back up unless there is a significant injury. An injury is an exception. The normal and expected occurrence is that players fall and get right back up. You need people on your team who know how to quickly recover when they feel like something has knocked them down. You need people on your team who know how to bounce back and keep going when they are hit with obstacles or make mistakes. You do not need people who experience a setback, and they decide to stay back. Falling down should never result in staying down. Life happens. When trials in life seem to knock us down, we must do everything within our power to get back up. This is the mindset that everyone on your team must have. In the words of legendary gospel singer and Pastor, Donnie McClurkin, "We fall down, but we get up."

HARD WORK OUTWEIGHS TALENT

The best soccer teams are made up of the hardest-working players. Talent can get you where only perseverance can keep you. There are a lot of talented soccer players who have either never made a team or who have been cut from a team simply because they rely solely on talent and ignore the value of arduous work. We must not negate arduous work. Even the most talented individuals get better when they commit themselves to working hard. Relying solely on talent can make us lazy and while we may be highly skilled, it can prevent us from becoming great. Oftentimes, good is the enemy of great. Why settle for good when you were designed to be great? You need people on your team who work hard. You deserve people on your team who are committed to being great over being good. Surround yourself with those who fully understand the value of arduous work.

Implementing these eight components taken from the game of soccer will provide you with what you need to form and establish the perfect team around you. Keep building, growing, and going, utilizing these tools and watch your team soar far beyond your biggest dreams. As it pertains to building a perfect team, it truly is, just like soccer.

A Moment of Reflection
Chapter 6: Life is Like Soccer: How to Build the Perfect Team

As you reflect on how "Life is Like Soccer," who do you currently know that possesses any of the qualities needed for being a member on your perfect team? What qualities (or individuals) are you missing on your team and how will you find those qualities or missing team members?

A Moment of Reflection

A Moment of Reflection

A Moment of Reflection

Chapter 7
LIFE IS LIKE TENNIS: HOW TO MAXIMIZE YOUR LIFE

*"So, teach us to number our days,
That we may gain a heart of wisdom." - Psalm 90:12 (NKJV)*

*"… being confident of this very thing, that He who has begun a good work in you
will complete it until the day of Jesus Christ." - Philippians 1:6 (NKJV)*

*"… whereas you do not know what will happen tomorrow. For what is your
life? It is even a vapor that appears for a little time and then vanishes away." -
James 4:14 (NKJV)*

When we consider the life and legacy of individuals, we must understand that it is not about their start date (the day they were born) or their end date (the day they died). It is about the dash in-between. God has given us a small window to accomplish each of the purposes and plans that He created us for. That window is represented by the dash between our start date and end date. The dash assigned to us is too small for it to be dominated by anger, resentment, bitterness, anxiety, discouragement, or any counter-productive emotion. While David wrote most of the Psalms, the Psalm listed above is actually written by Moses. In this Psalm, he is asking God to please help us be mindful of our limited time here on this side of life and, because of this mindfulness, maximize our time here by spending it being as wise as possible. In one of my favorite scriptures, Philippians 1:6, the Apostle Paul reminds us that God not only has a specific plan for our lives, but He began working that plan long before we became aware of our own existence. He encourages us to find confidence in the fact that He will continue to work that plan until the return of Jesus Christ. You must understand that you were created on purpose for a purpose. By no means were you an accident. Even if people did not expect you, God expected you. In fact, God made plans, pondering who would be perfect to accomplish His plans, thought about you, then created you. Jeremiah 1:5 lets us know that before God formed us in the womb, He knew us. What a deep truth. God had relationship with you before your mother and father had relationship with each other. It bears repeating, you were not and are not an accident. James 4:14 speaks to the truth that our life is but a short window, a dash. Therefore, the question we need to ask ourselves is, "How am I spending my dash? Am I truly maximizing my dash?"

The game of tennis teaches us a lot about how to maximize our dash; how to ensure that we are living our best life. Life is too short for you to compromise, settle, just get by, or barely manage. It is too short for you to be "moderately happy." God did not create you to be capricious in your emotions or just getting by, trying to make the best of it. You were not created to just accept whatever comes your way and try to console yourself with the old adage, "Well, it is what it is." You were not created just to pay bills and do the best that you can. You were created for greatness. Consider this, everything God does is great. He is a great God and only does remarkable things. The sun is great. The moon is great. The stars are great. Why? He is a great God. A great God who created a great sun, great moon, and impressive stars, did not get average when He created you. When God created you, He surpassed any other creation He made before you. You are the only creation who God declares is made in His image. You may resemble your mother or father, but you were made in God's image. That is the reason we must take ownership of the life that God has given us and maximize every bit of it. We must exhaust every aspect of it and live it to the fullest. Living your best life is not a pleasant thing, it is an expected thing.

There are seven lessons that I have learned from the game of tennis that, when applied to your life, will inevitably help you maximize your life. Let us dig in and see what they are.

SMALL WINS EQUAL BIG VICTORIES

Oftentimes, we underestimate the power of small victories. Being that we do not understand the power of small victories, we do not take the time to celebrate them. Too often we dismiss them as no big deal when in fact they are an incredibly big deal. The Bible asks in Zechariah 4:10, "For who has despised the day of small things?" While none of us would purposely raise our hand and say, "Me! I despise the day of small things!" Frequently, that is exactly the answer we give through our actions toward small victories. Whenever we say, "Oh, that's no big deal," we stand the chance of minimizing the importance of something that should be celebrated. Every small victory is significant. Every small victory is important.

In tennis, winning a single set does not win an entire match. However, winning multiple sets, more than your opponent, does win an entire match. In order to win a match, you must first win a set. Without victory in a set, there is no victory in a match. Life works the same way. There are no major victories in life without smaller wins. If your goal is to buy a house, you first must win in your employment and income. You must then win in your budgeting. You must also win in your credit. These smaller wins carry you to the extraordinary victory of homeownership. You cannot dismiss the importance of employment, budget, and credit because you are solely focused on buying a house.

If you are going to maximize your life, you must take the time to enjoy the small victories. Doing so brings a greater sense of awareness as to how blessed you really are. It also increases peace, passion, and productivity. Celebrating small victories increases a lifestyle of gratitude. A lifestyle of gratitude has proven benefits for everything from your ability to hope to maintaining optimal health.

One scripture that has always puzzled me is the one that David writes in Psalm 23:2 where he states, "He makes me lie down in green pastures." I have always read that and thought, "Why in the world does God have to make you lie down in green pastures? It would seem to me that if the pastures are green, you would want to lie down and, if anything, He would have to make you get up." Unfortunately, that is not what David's experience is and far too often that is not what our experience is either. In many cases, God must force us to lie down in green pastures. What do I mean? Often, we are so focused on what is next that we do not or cannot enjoy what already is. Sometimes, God must slow us down so that we can enjoy our current blessings. We are not blessed because of what we are going to get. We are blessed because of what we already have. If you really want to start enjoying and maximizing your life, make up in your mind that you will not let another accomplishment or victory that you would normally categorize as "no big deal" happen without you stopping to celebrate it. Celebrate everything and watch the spirit of your life get better.

CONSTANTLY LEARN

You may be surprised to know that tennis players often say that tennis is far more mental than physical. Obviously, it is very physical, however, it is far more mental. In fact, I have heard it said that tennis is approximately 80% more mental than physical. Tennis players are always evaluating and re-evaluating, calculating, and re-calculating. They are always studying the game, gaining new tools to add to their tool chest. They are always learning new ways to approach the game. They are always expanding their mind. They are always seeking to expand their level of wisdom. Tennis players create a lifetime of learning. Their desire to constantly learn is what helps them constantly adjust to the nature of the game or opponent. The game is constantly shifting on some level, and so being a student of the game allows talented players to shift with the game. The best tennis players continue to study and learn so that they might remain among the best.

The reality is, no one can continue to be among the best at anything if they do not commit to a lifestyle of continual study, learning, and evolving. In life, we must be a student of life. We must constantly seek to learn and gain wisdom. We must constantly seek to expand our mind. People often fight what they do not understand, and oftentimes, once they understand it, they want to fight themselves for taking so long to embrace what they are now able to utilize. I can remember some of the old school church folks speaking against going to the movies and watching television. Years later, many of them wanted to appear in a movie or on television. What if instead of fighting and speaking against viewing television and going to the movies, they would have made the decision to embrace and learn it back then. Perhaps many would have owned a television station or movie studio instead of hoping to get recognized by one.

The Bible states in Proverbs 4:7, "Wisdom is the principal thing; therefore, get wisdom. And in all your getting, get understanding."

If you want to maximize your life, then become a person who is always learning. Every month should culminate with you having researched, studied, read, and learned something that will help take your life to the next level. Whatever your goal is in life, do not ever stop learning about it. Individuals often tell me that they have a "burning desire" to do something. My response is always, "Success comes when your burning is accompanied and complimented by your learning." Live a life of constant learning.

DO NOT STOP MOVING

Anyone who has ever watched a tennis match can attest to the fact that the players are constantly moving. There is no telling where the opponent is going to hit the ball. Therefore, players are constantly running from side to side and front to back. Standing still does absolutely nothing but speed up defeat. Life is the same way. We must make sure that we are always moving. Let me be clear and say, we must always be moving with purpose. Moving just to move does nothing. Tennis players move because they are trying to get to the ball. All your movement should be in the direction of your goal. If the moves you are making do not push you toward your goal, then those are the wrong moves. Every move you make should place you another step closer to your goal. Attending a conference, seminar, or workshop on whatever subject that is related to your goal is an example of making good moves. Connecting with people who have experienced success in the field you desire success in, is making a good move. Investing time and money to help get you closer to your goal is making a good move. I could name several other items, but you get my point. Every day, make a move that pushes you in the direction of your goal.

You can save yourself a ton of time and headache if you remember and abide by the words in Proverbs 3:6, "In all your ways acknowledge Him [God], and He shall direct your paths." Always start with talking to God. Do what I do. I always ask God to make His desire and direction for my life so clear that it would be impossible for me to miss it, and He does exactly that every single time. God knows how to get your attention and speak your language. You just need to ask Him then, be on the lookout for His response.

Keep making productive moves and watch your life become more enjoyable. You are never too old or too young to make a move. If you woke up this morning, you have moves to make.

OWN YOUR HEALTH

Tennis players must be healthy. There is no way they can do all the moving and shifting that they do and not be healthy. If they are not healthy, it shows in their game. Do you know that life is more enjoyable when you are healthy? The Apostle John wrote in 3 John 1:2, "Beloved, I pray that you may prosper in all things and be in health, just as your soul prospers." God wants us to be healthy. He can use us better when we are healthy. He can use us longer when we are healthy. Too many people have such amazing gifts and talents but cannot fully maximize them because they are not taking care of their bodies. Moses walked up and down the mountain, carrying heavy tablets. He had to be healthy. Noah built an ark. He had to be healthy. David fought a lion, a bear, and a giant named Goliath, and conquered all of them. He had to be healthy. I could go on and on, but the greatest men and women of the Bible were those who took care of their bodies. If there is one thing, I strongly encourage people to do, it is to take care of their bodies. We only have one body, and we have a responsibility to protect it. Be mindful of what you eat. You can enjoy dining out and even eating what you want, however, the key is to be responsible. The key for you is moderation. Indulge in fast food on the weekend because you have done so well eating healthy all week. Commit to exercising and some form of movement. Perhaps take a walk in the mornings, afternoons, or evenings - whatever your schedule allows. Make it a prayer walk where you just talk to God the entire time. You can make it a friend's walk, strolling with a good friend discussing your dreams and goals. Perhaps it is a music walk, listening to your favorite music artists as you tread down your pathway. It is your job to own your health. You must take ownership of it and in the words of my dear friend, Bebe Winans, "Get it done."

RELEASE STRESS

Many tennis players have told me how tennis is the perfect stress releaser. As they run, shift, adjust, swing the racket, and hit the ball, stress is being released. We must find methods to release the stress that is in our lives. The bottom line is stress is so dangerous that it can take a toll on your health and be a silent killer. Stress causes severe health problems. In addition to causing severe physical problems, stress causes severe emotional and psychological problems as well. I cannot stress enough how detrimental stress is for us. We must take every measure that we can to reduce stress. Sometimes circumstances cause stress and sometimes it is a person causing the stress. Do not allow people to stress you out. Set boundaries and stick to them. Unhealthy people do not like healthy boundaries. Set them anyway. If possible, disconnect from people who produce tension in your life. Learn how to love them from a distance. If, for some reason, you cannot fully disconnect from them, then set boundaries with them and be incredibly open and honest about the level of stress that they produce in your life. If it is a certain component stressing you out, create a game plan to overcome that thing. A good game plan fixes everything. You may need help creating a game plan. If you need help, read the chapter "Life is like Soccer" and build a team that will help you overcome your stressful obstacle. Everything can be overcome.

Do not let stress keep you from enjoying your life. Life is not easy but manage your stress. Do not let life happen to you. You happen to life. Be proactive. Take time to travel out of town whenever possible. Go for a drive. Take a vacation to a different city, country, or a staycation right in the same city, or even in your house. Take a break. You owe it to yourself to take a break and pamper yourself. Do something for you. Treat yourself. Reward yourself. Bottom line, love yourself.

Stress is your enemy. Do not allow things that you cannot control to control you. Here is a free motto that I will give you to live by. Tell yourself, "I am going to stress less and function at my best." Now do not just say it, do whatever you need to do to make it a reality.

RESPECT EVERYONE

Remarkable tennis players know that their opponents must be respected. They keep in mind that the other person is standing on the opposite side of the court for a particularly good reason. To not respect their opponent would be a disrespect to themselves. When they respect their opponent, they play responsibly. When they respect their opponent, they treat them differently and view them differently. Respect causes them to treat them as an equal. Respect causes them to acknowledge the fact that their opponent also possesses gifts and talents. Respect causes them to recognize that their opponent also has a skill set. They do not take their opponent for granted. They take them very seriously. The more they respect their opponent, the better they play. The more they respect their opponent, the greater chance they have of winning. In life, we must respect everyone. When we respect everyone, life inevitably improves for us. The best way to respect everyone is to remember that God created everyone just like He created you. Therefore, everyone is God's son or daughter. Even if they do not act like it, it does not change the fact that they are God's creation. Many of us have family members who do not behave like they are in the same family as everyone else, so, understand that God's family is the same way. There are many people who do not act properly, but God still created them. You will never look into the eyes of an individual who was not made in the image of God. Everyone was made in His image. I did not say everyone presents themselves like they were made in His image. I simply said that everyone was. Remembering that everyone was created by God, will certainly help you respect everyone whom you encounter. Please note, that respecting someone does not mean being close friends or spending time with them. Respecting someone simply means to treat them kindly by accepting them for who they are. Everyone deserves love and respect. Make it part of your mission to show love and respect to everyone and watch your life get better as a result.

COMMIT FOR A LIFETIME

Tennis is one of those rare sports that I have witnessed people play throughout their entire lifetime. I have seen some incredibly young players and some incredibly seasoned players playing the game with such enthusiasm. Tennis will forever be a game for all ages. It is for that reason, that many players make a lifetime commitment to the game, especially the amateurs that play the game for pure recreational purposes. Our commitment to life should be a lifetime commitment. We should have a lifetime commitment to learning, growing, striving, thriving, reaching, teaching, and loving. The sour days should never cause us to quit because we have a lifetime commitment to success, joy, happiness, and peace. Life is made up of highs and lows, successes, and teaching moments, but our lifetime commitment should cause us to continue moving forward and enjoying life. Commit to this God-given journey for a lifetime and enjoy the journey. Learn all that you can. Enjoy all that you can. Produce all that you can. This life, your life, is such a precious gift. In case no one has told you, you are such a precious gift from God to all of us. Please commit to maximizing your life, not just today or temporarily, but for a lifetime. Do not give up. Do not walk away. Do not admit defeat. Remember, if you are not where you want to be, get a game plan and you will immediately be closer today than you were yesterday. We need you to keep going. Everyone around you needs you to commit to this thing called life, for a lifetime.

It is amazing how the tips of tennis can help us maximize every aspect of our lives if we just apply them. You were created for greatness. Accomplish everything that you were created for by applying these seven tips from tennis and making the decision that you are going to maximize your life.

A Moment of Reflection
Chapter 7: Life is Like Tennis: How to Maximize Your Life

As you reflect on how "Life is Like Tennis," what area(s) of your life need to be deliberately tended to so that you are better able to maximize your life?

A Moment of Reflection

A Moment of Reflection

A Moment of Reflection

Chapter 8
LIFE IS LIKE TRACK AND FIELD: HOW TO FINISH WHAT YOU HAVE STARTED

"But now you also must complete the doing of it; that as there was a readiness to desire it, so there also may be a completion out of what you have."
- 2 Corinthians 8:11 (NKJV)

One of the all-time greatest motivational speakers, Les Brown, once said, "The graveyard is the richest place on earth because it is here that you will find all the hopes and dreams that were never fulfilled, the books that were never written, the songs that were never sung, the inventions that were never shared, the cures that were never discovered, all because someone was too afraid to take that first step, keep with the problem, or determined to carry out their dream." These words are not just filled with incredible truth but should serve as motivation for each of us to do a self-evaluation and ask ourselves if we may fall in danger of being a contributing statistic to this fact. Too many people have had life-changing ideas yet failed to see them through to completion. Too many of us have started and stopped something repeatedly and spent years trying to complete something that could have been done in half of the amount of time that we have already spent. If this is you, please do not stop now. Keep going and finish. We often have many reasons, which are completely understandable, as to why we have not or do not finish what we have started. Major life changes or transitions, workloads, family responsibilities, financial problems, health issues, and many other real-life occurrences often put our passions on the back burner. Unfortunately, too many of us have simply been victims of procrastination. Unbelievably, procrastinators are not careless or lethargic people. In fact, being careless is often not connected to why individuals procrastinate. Many of the reasons why individuals procrastinate will be dealt with in this chapter as we look at how life is like track and field. It is much easier to finish what you have started when you can truly see its value. When you can truly see the difference that will be made in the lives of people or even in your own life, you will find yourself using that as motivation. It is easy to not finish something that is pointless. However, that is not what many of us are guilty of. Many of us are guilty of not finishing something that would be a game changer for society. You must understand that someone around you needs you to finish what you have started. God has placed something on your heart for someone who has been seeking Him for answers. Your idea or project is God's answer to someone's prayer request. Remember that and finish.

As my wife and I attended our kids' track and field events, I quickly discovered how the events offer nine lessons on how to finish what we have started in life. Too excited to keep these track and field life-changing gems to myself, I decided that I had to share them with you.

RUN YOUR RACE

Track and field consist of multiple events, both on the track and on the field. There are over forty events that can occur during a track and field meet, causing the meets to last for several hours. Being that track and field has several different events and can last for so long, it has become the most contested of any sport. This is particularly noticeable during the Olympics. Several different events mean several different choices that athletes must make as they consider the capacity in which they will compete. Considering there are so many different choices to make, athletes must ensure that they choose the event that is best suited for them. They want to select the event that highlights their strengths and abilities the most. The most options are presented to runners. Runners have the option to choose everything from short distance sprints to long distance marathons. It is for that reason that runners must be careful to choose the event that helps them run their race. Just because someone is a great long-distance runner does not mean they will be a great 100-meter sprinter, and just because someone is a great 100-meter sprinter does not mean they will be a great long-distance runner. Therefore, runners must carefully determine the type of run that maximizes and highlights their running talent. Such is life. Life presents us with several options to elect from. We must choose the option that best highlights our gifts and talents. Even better than running track, there is a God-given path that is customized just for you. We must do all that we can to find that path and "run it" with all our might. Many of us do not finish what we have started because we have yet to discover the path that God has designed for us. We have tried several paths and have found ourselves either quitting or lagging unusually far behind simply because the race that we are running is not our race. Our race is our journey. Our race is our calling. We are fully motivated once we find ourselves living out our calling through our journey. You must run your race. You cannot run the race someone has forced you into. You must run the race for which you were created. You cannot run the race the way someone else would run it. You must run your race the way God has created you to run it. You cannot be manipulated into a race that was designed for someone else. You must run your race. I cannot stress enough how important it is to run your race; the one that not only highlights your strengths, abilities, talents, and gifts but also brings the most fulfillment and joy. The race that was designed for you satisfies you in a way that no other race can. Your race is your purpose.

Let me give you a priceless tip on how to locate your race, or purpose. Your race, or purpose, is connected to what makes you upset when it is done wrong. The reason it upsets you is because you are called to see it done right. You were created to be part of the solution. You are the change you have been wishing to see. The change that you hope for, is your race.

STAY IN YOUR LANE

You have probably either said the phrase, "Stay in your lane," to or about someone, or it has been said to or about you. Nothing is worse than a runner, running in someone else's lane. When a runner runs in another runner's lane, they not only hurt their own race, but they hurt the other runner's race as well. Inevitably, unless adjustments are made for everyone to return to their own lane, the entire race is hurt. In life, it is important that we stay in our lane. This does not just mean to avoid involving yourself in matters that do not pertain to you. This means being true to your authentic self. To be true to your authentic self, you must know and have confidence in the fact that God has already equipped you to get from where you are to the next place you need to be. That is a constant truth. In every stage of life, you will always have what you need to get from where you are to the next place that you need, or desire to be. Whenever you need more, you will have more. However, rest assured that in the meantime, you have everything that you need to accomplish whatever needs to be accomplished to get to the next stage or phase of your journey to achieving your God-given purpose.

When David prepared to fight Goliath, Saul urged David to use all his equipment. David told Saul that he could not because that equipment was not how God had given him to fight Goliath. Even if another person's resources, ideas, and plans sound great and have worked perfectly for them, we must walk in the path that is true to who God made us. You can admire someone and still be your authentic self. Admiring does not have to mean imitating. Admiring should never mean copying. You can have inspiration without imitation. Be true to who God made you to be and stay in your lane. When you do this, you have a greater chance of finishing what you started because you do not become burned out trying to keep up with something that God never intended for you to apply to yourself. It is much easier to keep going when you are going in your authentic self. The authentic you can last much longer than the imitation you.

KEEP YOUR EYES ON THE FINISH LINE

Every time a runner looks over at another runner or looks behind themselves, they take time off their run. Every turn away from the finish line subtly affects their posture and overall pace, slowing down the time in which they can finish. The most unfortunate part about it, is that this slowdown is not usually noticeable. However, it has been the cause of many runners not finishing within the time they could have finished. In life, we must do all that we can to keep our eyes on the finish line. Once you have a goal and make a plan, focus solely on that. Distractions will come, however, every glance at a distraction has a negative effect on your progress. How do you know if something is a distraction? You know when it holds zero benefit for your journey. As I have stated before, things either help you or they hurt you. They do not partially help you nor do they partially hurt you. It is one or the other. Therefore, once you can categorize something as not helping you, you can also categorize it as a distraction. Now, with that being said, it is worth noting that oftentimes things that are helping you do not feel pleasant, however, they are helping you. Sometimes situations or circumstances are not pleasing, but they produce much needed growth in a certain area of your life. The best way to find out if something that does not feel good is actually helping you, is to ask yourself the question, "What am I supposed to learn from this?" If you can answer that question with something that makes you better, though it was unpleasant, it still worked out for your good. At the end of the day, the goal is to continue keeping your eyes on the finish line. Where are you headed? How close are you? Focus forward. When you keep your eyes on the finish line, it is easier to stay motivated because you see the end. You see the big picture. You see the goal. You see the value in completing. Do not ever let anything have more of your attention than your ultimate goal. Blocking out distractions, refusing to be pre-occupied with what others are doing, and refusing to look behind you will serve in a major way in helping you finish what you have started.

OVERCOME THE HURDLES

I admire hurdlers. They have a pathway full of obstacles that they must jump over. Not just one or two, but several. Hurdlers somehow prepare their minds and their bodies to jump over every obstacle that is in their path. It is every bit of a mental, physical, and emotional game. They first must overcome any negative mental thought that would try to defeat them before they even leave the blocks. Fear must be overcome. Anxiety must be overcome. Doubt must be overcome. There must be a victory in their mind before there is a victory in their race. Physically, they must know exactly where to jump, how to jump, where to land, and how to land. They must know the right pace, the perfect extension of their legs, and the overall perfect movements for their entire body. There is a lot of physical wisdom that must go into properly jumping a hurdle. Emotionally, it is imperative they remain calm and connected to an inner peace. With the right mental, physical, and emotional position they can overcome every hurdle that is in their way. Hurdles that come up in everyday life are no different. It is necessary that we position ourselves mentally, physically, and emotionally to overcome every hurdle that is in our path. There is no hurdle that you will ever face, that you cannot overcome. The question will always be whether or not you are willing to do the work that is needed mentally, physically, and emotionally to jump over the hurdle. Hurdles come, but when you are applying the things that we have already talked about, you do what you need to do to jump over it. While it is good to know why a hurdle is there so that you do not repeat the same mistakes, do not get so consumed with trying to figure out why the hurdle is there that you neglect doing what you need to do to overcome it. Having a mindset to jump over any hurdles that appear in your path will keep you moving forward toward your goal and help you finish what you have started.

PACE YOURSELF

Long distance runners understand that the key to finishing well is recognizing the value of a consistent pace over speed. It is impossible for a runner to keep up a fast speed or full-blown sprint for the entire time in a long-distance race. You often see runners increase their speed as they are nearing the end, but you do not see that end speed in the beginning and maintained the entire time. For long distance runners, it is more about pace. When they pace themselves, they have greater stamina, better breathing, clearer focus, and stronger determination. The decision to pace themselves is the best decision that they can make mentally, physically, and emotionally. Pacing themselves ensures that they are not so quickly or easily burned out. Pacing themselves is all about a commitment to longevity over quick finish. Many of us have not finished what we have started because we have not learned to pace ourselves. We started a project on fire with plenty of unprecedented energy but then quickly ran out of gas because we prioritized speed over pace. Frequently, this is done on a subconscious level. We may not be aware that this is what we are doing, but it is confirmed when we make statements like, "It's taking too long" or, "It took too long, so I stopped." Great achievements take time. You cannot rush game-changing achievements. Pace yourself and stick with your endeavor. In order to properly pace yourself, you must build in breaks to refresh and recover. It is far better to finish right, healthy, and strong than to finish fast. Pacing yourself helps you keep the momentum that you need to finish what you have started.

PUSH THROUGH

There comes a time in every long-distance runner's life where they feel like they have run out of gas. It is during these moments that it is necessary they learn how to push through the feeling of not having any more to give. Their breathing becomes crucial. Their ability to focus becomes a major factor in overcoming this feeling of being in over their head and not having anything left to help them reach the finish line. It becomes a matter of mental, emotional, and physical strength. Then, at some point, they dig down deep within themselves and find the necessary strength needed to push through and continue going forward. Life is the same way. All of us will experience seasons in life where we feel overwhelmed. We will all experience moments when we want to give up, when we have run out of gas, in over our head, up against the wall, or like we cannot do anymore. All these thoughts and feelings are normal. I would even say that each of these thoughts and feelings are expected. However, it is in these moments that we need to discover the strength needed to push through. If you can just push through the challenging times, you will be surprised to identify what is waiting for you on the other side. Everyone wants the success, but few want to do the work. The challenging part is pushing through the very moment that gives you the perfect opportunity or excuse to opt out. If you can just push through the moment when you want to give up, then you can finish what you have started. Push through and finish; seeing your dream become a reality is worth the extra push.

PASSING THE BATON

I love watching the relay race. There are so many lessons to be learned. There are lessons on teamwork and lessons on staying focused. However, I think one of the most powerful and valuable lessons come when you watch and consider the actual passing of the baton. It matters who is passing the baton and it matters those to whom the baton is being passed. Those connected to passing or receiving the baton must be incredibly aware and athletic. The relay is the ultimate in seeing the relationship between awareness and athleticism. The two certainly go hand in hand in the relay. The runners positioned between the first runner and the last runner have two crucial questions to ask themselves. Those questions are, "Who is passing me the baton and who am I passing the baton to?" Those same two questions become crucial to us as we pursue the journey and goals that God has given us. It is impossible to have clear direction on where you need to go if you do not have a clear understanding on where you have come from. Consider yourself having a baton in your hand with a leg of a race to run for your family's legacy. Now ask yourself, "Who passed you this baton?" In other words, what is the history behind you becoming who you are today? This does not mean you have to know or have a personal relationship with everyone in your immediate lineage. However, this does mean doing your best to understand how you got on the journey that you are currently on. There is a

baton in your hand. How did it get there? What is it for? Where are you called to carry it? There is a leg of a legacy that has been handed to you. Think about that for a moment. You are here to run a leg of a legacy. Where did the legacy come from? What is your assignment for this leg of the journey? And, further-more, when you have finished your part of the race, who are you to hand the baton to? Everyone has been strategically placed to both receive and impart. What have you received? What will you do with what you have received? Then, how will your management of what you have received affect what you impart? You were created to get something and give something. What is that something? When you discover the answers to these questions, you will find it easier to finish what was started long before you. Do not drop the baton. Run your leg of your family's legacy.

PICK IT UP AND CAST IT AS FAR AS POSSIBLE

Whether we are talking about the discus, javelin, shot put, or hammer throw, the idea behind them all is to grab the specified object and cast it as far away from you as you can. The athlete's form and techniques may vary slightly but, the goal remains the same across the board. Athletes may have different means by which they build momentum but again, the goal is the same. The Bible states in Hebrews 12:1b, "…let us lay aside every weight, and the sin which so easily ensnares us, and let us run with endurance the race that is set before us." We must grab hold to everything that weighs us down and holds us back and launch them as far away from us as possible. We must make every effort to release and disconnect from anything that is working against us or hindering our journey to our eventual goal. Once you discover what your ultimate goal is, you must then determine to cast away anything that does not help you achieve that goal. Discard it as far away from you as possible. And, once you cast it away, leave it there. Do not, under any circumstances, go and retrieve the very item that you have already decided needed to be cast away. The more you eliminate unpro-ductive weights, the greater your chances are of finishing what you have started.

USE WHAT YOU HAVE TO GO HIGHER

Of all the events that track and field have to offer, the pole vault is by far one of the most fascinating to me. I am thoroughly intrigued and amazed at how the athletes can take a pole and perfectly position it onto the ground in such a way to where it launches them high into the air and over the bar that is in front of them. This is quite amazing to me. It is not like they are wearing a jet pack or bouncing shoes. It is a pole that bends. Somehow, they manage to use what they have to go as high as they need to go in order to rise above the obstacle that is in their way. This is a major life lesson for all of us. Many of us are waiting for more tools to assist us in obtaining the next level in life. However, I have already told you that you have everything you need to get from where you are to the next place that you need to be. You do not need any more resources right now. You need to use what you already have. Whether we are watching the Wizard of Oz or The Wiz, we will discover that everything the main characters were looking for, they already had. The scarecrow already had a brain, the tin man already had a heart, the lion already had courage, and Dorothy already had her answer on her feet. Biblically speaking, God used the rod that was already in Moses' hand to deliver the children of Israel out of Pharaoh's hand. Your next move is not to acquire more possessions. Your next move is to ask God to help you maximize what you already have. You are enough and you have enough. Use what you currently possess to get from where you are to where you need to be. Build from the foundation that you already laid. Use your current skillset, gifts, talents, abilities, and resources, and make up in your mind that you are going to go higher. Every night ask yourself this question, "Am I further along tonight than I was yesterday?" Do everything within your power to make that answer a "Yes" every single night. Use what you have and go higher.

I firmly believe that if we utilize these nine lessons that track and field teaches us, we will not only finish what we have started but, when we come to the end of our journey, we will be able to proclaim the same words that the Apostle Paul proclaims in 2 Timothy 4:7, "I have fought the good fight, I have finished the race, I have kept the faith." Own these nine lessons and finish what you have started.

A Moment of Reflection
Chapter 8: Life is Like Track and Field:
How to Finish What You Have Started

As you reflect on how "Life is Like Track and Field," is there any area, projected goal in your life that you started but never finished? As you decide to return to it and finish it, what steps will you implement to ensure that you complete it this time around?

A Moment of Reflection

A Moment of Reflection

A Moment of Reflection

Chapter 9
LIFE IS LIKE GYMNASTICS: HOW TO GROW FORWARD

"Not that I speak in regard to need, for I have learned in whatever state I am, to be content: I know how to be abased, and I know how to abound. Everywhere and in all things, I have learned both to be full and to be hungry, both to abound and to suffer need. I can do all things through Christ who strengthens me."
- Philippians 4:11-13 (NKJV)

Life is all about consistent growth. To be consistent in our growth, we must remain aware of our growth. Even if you do not have everything that you desire, the important question is, "Have you grown?" You may not have all the money that you yearn for, the car that you wish for, the house that you have your heart set on, the job that you want, or the relationship that you desire, but have you grown? Have you grown emotionally? Have you grown spiritually? Have you grown mentally? If you have grown, then you are still living a productive life. Even if you do not know what to do, at least let growth teach you what you do not want to do. You may not know who you want to date, but at least you know who you do not want to date. That is growth. The Apostle Paul's statement in the scripture at the start of this chapter shows incredible growth. Apostle Paul states that he is learned, which means he is grown. He is grown spiritually, emotionally, and mentally. He is grown to the point of being able to remain satisfied no matter what he is dealing with. He is truly clear to let us know that he is only able to do that because of his relationship with Jesus Christ. He is clear that on his own he would not be in the place of contentment that he is in. He is clear that he is in that place because he gains strength (courage, durability, and stability) by relying on Jesus Christ for all the help that he needs to survive with whatever he is dealing. As a result, he is constantly learning and constantly growing. We should all make it our goal to live a life of this kind of nonstop growth.

I discovered the keys to finding this kind of constant and solid growth as I watched gymnastics. The bare fundamentals of gymnastics gave me five things that will help us grow forward in life.

BELIEVE

Before a gymnast can perform any routine, they must first believe that they can do it. Confidence is an absolute must. There can be no room left for fear. Fear will only work against them. They must believe that they have what it takes and that they are well able and equipped to perform the task that lies ahead. They need to be the number one believer in themselves. They must believe in themselves before anyone else does. Self-confidence lays the foundation for accomplishments. Therefore, success in their particular performance begins in their belief in themselves. Life for us is the same. Success begins or ends in what you believe; specifically, and most importantly, what you believe about yourself. After having a solid belief in God, you then must believe in yourself. This belief in yourself is not one of arrogance, but rather one of confidence. Arrogance is the result of crediting yourself with what God has done with and in you. Confidence is the result of knowing it is God who did it and deserves all the credit for the things that He is continuing to do in and with you, then trusting Him with yourself. This confidence starts with believing who and what God made when He made you. The truth is, when you know whose, you are, you discover and become confident in who you are. As a result, if you believe that you can, then you can. If you believe that you cannot, then you cannot. It all starts with what you believe.

Every time I talk about believing in oneself, I think of an experiment that was done with a flea in a jar. The flea spent some time in a jar with a lid on it. Whenever the flea would jump, it would hit the lid. After a while, the flea was conditioned to believe that it could not get out of the jar because there was a lid there. Finally, the lid was removed but guess what? Even though the flea could now jump out of the jar, it would not jump out of the jar. Why? It was still under the belief that there was a lid there. This belief was preventing it from jumping out of the jar even though it was now possible. Too many of us have the ability to go beyond where we feel stuck or limited but have been conditioned to believe that there is something that will stop us. Unfortunately, this conditioning is the result of past experiences that have left us feeling confined, defined, or bound by unpleasant or uncertain circumstances. However, despite any negative conditioning that your past may have on your present, I want you to know that with God all things are possible, and you have the support and freedom in Him to go beyond any place you have ever gone before. God has removed the lid out of your life. The Apostle Paul said, "I can do all things through Christ who strengthens me." This includes soaring past the very thing that made you feel stuck. Believe that you can and do it.

There is a powerful statement made in Numbers 13:33 after a group of the children of Israel traveled to scout out a land that God told them He had already given to them. After scouting out the land, a few of them reported back and said, "...and we were like grasshoppers in our own sight, and so we were in their sight." They speak these words of defeat, after God have already confirmed to them that they would have victory. Fear is immensely powerful and can cause you to miss blessings that God has already set up for you. You need to know that you are whatever you believe you are. It is also worth noting that the people in the land saw the children of Israel as grasshoppers because the children of Israel saw themselves as grasshoppers. People tend to see you how you see yourself. Through your view of yourself, you shape people's perception of you and what they believe about you.

Believe in yourself by knowing that you did not create yourself, but that God created you. Believe that God made a great person when He made you. Believe that God has equipped you and believe that God believes in you. If you believe these things, you will be believing the truth, and this truth will help you grow forward.

BALANCE

Even if they are not competing on the balance beams, gymnasts must still master the art of balance. Their ability to balance becomes the difference between accurately executing their routine and making mistakes that cost them when the judges score their routine. Every routine that a gymnast performs requires balance. You cannot be a great gymnast and lack balance. While you and I may not be gymnasts, we must still practice balance. Success in life requires mastering the art of balance. Working hard must be balanced with self-care. Business relationships must be balanced with personal friendships. Investments must be balanced with saving. Even exercise must be balanced with recovery. Life requires balance. Work hard but enjoy a vacation as well. Individuals who live a balanced life are not so easily overwhelmed or burned out because they know how to retreat, refresh, recover, and re-engage when necessary. A one-sided life in any direction is not a healthy life because it is not a balanced life. An unhealthy life is not a life being used and enjoyed to the fullest. An unhealthy life or unbalanced life is truly an incomplete life. It is a life lacking all that God has for us. I believe in working hard but I also believe in family vacations. I believe in attending seminars, workshops, and conferences that produce much needed growth, but I believe in attending our children's school events as well. I believe in meeting with other Pastors because I am a Pastor, but I believe in meeting with my children's teachers because I am a father as well. Life is all about balance. Balance will keep you functioning on a healthy level and keep you mentally, emotionally, spiritually, and physically engaged. Balance will keep you motivated. Balancing will work against burn out. Balance will keep you growing forward.

CREATIVITY

If you watch gymnastics, you know that it is all about creativity. Scores are based on a gymnast's ability to think outside of the box, go against the norm, and execute a creative routine. The more creative the routine, the better the score. The most creative gymnast is the one that believes that if they can think it then they can do it. Their mind is not confined to only what they have seen work before. They think beyond the history and experiences of the sport and think about how to connect their present to their future by doing something that has never been done before. If we are going to grow forward in life, we need to think beyond our own experiences and history and think of options without limitations that will connect our present to our preferred future. What would you do if you knew it was impossible to fail? Start working that plan right there. Unfortunately, most people grow out of creativity not into creativity. Too many of our most creative years were our childhood years. As children, we did not know nor consider limitations. As children, we never thought of being stopped or something not working. We would make indoor forts that we were so proud to display out of blankets. We would make miniature model homes from a deck of cards. We would slide down the staircase in a laundry basket pretending to be on a roller coaster. We would pretend to be doctors, law enforcement officers, astronauts, rock stars, actors, and even superheroes. We thoroughly enjoyed it all because we had no sense of something not being possible. Over time, people and circumstances crushed some of our dreams and beliefs, but what if you took a moment to believe again? If you could believe again, you would discover that the creativity still lives on the inside of you. Creativity never left you. If anything, you left creativity. Look at what God has placed on the inside of you. It is still there. Think bigger. Plan bigger. Work bigger. Think outside of the box. Ignore statistics. Ignore opinions. Ignore history. Ignore everything you have been shown and told for one second. With a fresh and unfiltered perspective, think the wildest, out of the box, most creative life-changing, game changing thought that you can think. If you can think it, you can do it. Now get to work one step at a time. You might not be able to do everything all at once, but you can do something right now. Be creative and grow forward.

CONSISTENCY

Gymnasts do not perfectly perform every single time. Sometimes it is a masterpiece of a performance and sometimes there are major mistakes made. Being an exceptional gymnast is not about perfect execution every time. It is about maximum effort but not perfect execution. More than anything, it is about consistency. It is about the gymnast making up in their mind that they will show up, give their all, and keep trying no matter what happens. Great gymnasts fall, but they get back up and go for it again. They make mistakes but they take it again. They understand that endless effort and consistency is key to becoming a great, and eventually legendary, gymnast. Consistency feeds on determination. The most consistent gymnast is the most determined gymnast. Success in life comes because of consistency. Consistency is the byproduct of determination. If you want it bad enough, you keep trying. Even if it does not work the first time or several times, your determination to get it to work feeds your ability to be consistent. Determination is internal while consistency is external. Determination is that drive on the inside to see it happen. Consistency is that action on the outside to make it happen. Consistency separates the average person from the great person. Consistency leads to breakthrough. Consistency leads to resources and opportunities. Consistency will put you before people who can help you get what you have never gotten before. Consistency always gets noticed. Consistency is a major trait in growing forward. If you want to see growth in your life on multiple levels, just remain consistent. I have seen people consistently doing something that others told them they should stop doing because it was not working, suddenly have a major breakthrough moment and achieve what they hoped to achieve one day. Sometimes we look at people and mislabel them as "an overnight success." Nothing could be further from the truth. Just because we may have just heard of them, does not mean that they are an overnight success. We have no idea how many underground or behind the scenes countless hours of consistency went into finally getting their recognition. Never diminish someone's success to being overnight. Nothing is overnight. We may not have seen someone's consistent efforts before the big breakout, but trust me, the consistency was there. You do not have success without consistency. Be consistent and watch how growing forward becomes inevitable.

INDEPENDENCE

After all the teaching, training, mentoring, and coaching is done, it is up to the gymnast to own their event. Even with tremendous support, the events themselves tests the gymnast's ability to act independently. No one can flip, turn, twist, or move the body of the gymnast once it is performance time. The gymnast must remember everything that has led to this moment of independence and use it to show that they can execute on their own. In life, we have mentors, coaches, teachers, education, and a host of other resources and tools that prepare us to take certain actions in life. However, no one can do the actual work for us. At some point, we must show independence and execute the work for ourselves. People can open doors for us and do many things to set us up for success, but we must take ownership of our lives and build our future from our present situation. The more we learn to act independently, the more we grow. Too many people wait for someone to do something for them. We need to learn to create our own platforms and opportunities. Too many of us are waiting for someone to open a door for us. We need to create our own doors. This is what it means to take initiative. Working independently and taking initiative means being proactive. It means to maximize the knowledge that you have. People can give you knowledge, but it is up to you to use it. If you want to live a life that is growing forward, you must learn to work independently from time to time. Take the guidance and knowledge that you have already been given through multiple resources and move forward in that. Add independent research on what you would like to see happen in your life to the resources you have already been given and give yourself direction on moving forward. Working independently inevitably positions you for growing forward.

Create a life of being better every day. A life of consistent growth. Use these five traits that I learned by watching gymnastics and begin living a life that is never stagnant, boring, unproductive, or stale because it is constantly growing forward.

A Moment of Reflection
Chapter 9: Life is Like Gymnastics: How to Grow Forward

As you reflect on how "Life is Like Gymnastics," in what areas of your life have you experienced the most personal growth? In what areas of your life are you currently growing? In what areas of your life do you desire growth?

A Moment of Reflection

A Moment of Reflection

A Moment of Reflection

Chapter 10
LIFE IS LIKE VOLLEYBALL: HOW TO BE A GREAT LEADER

"So, he shepherded them according to the integrity of his heart,
And guided them by the skillfulness of his hands."
- Psalm 78:72 (NKJV)

"Let nothing be done through selfish ambition or conceit, but in lowliness of
mind let each esteem others better than himself. Let each of you look out not only
for his own interests, but also for the interests of others."
- Philippians 2:3-4 (NKJV)

Volleyball is certainly one of those sports that keeps me on the edge of my seat. The nonstop back and forth action between teams leading up to that big unpredictable moment where one teammate sets another teammate up for the scary, fast, and powerful spike. The adrenaline rush continues when the spike is quickly kept from being a point scored and instead countered with a spike from the opposing team. What an exhilarating sport to watch. I absolutely love volleyball. If you study the game of volleyball closely, you will discover six traits that every player must have to make a championship team. While volleyball is a team sport, the best teams are made up of individuals who possess certain leadership qualities. I have studied these leadership qualities and discovered that they apply to anyone who is looking to be the best leader that they can be. Anyone desiring to grow in leadership can study the traits found in skilled volleyball players and use them for that desired growth. Let me just say that everyone is a leader on some level. You may not be a business owner, employer, manager, human resources representative, or supervisor on your job, but you are a leader in some capacity in life. Perhaps you are a leader within your household. Maybe you are a leader within your family, within a community or church group. Perhaps you are a leader in your neighborhood. The list goes on and on. The truth is you were born a leader. God creates leaders. Sometimes that is the reason you do not fit in all the time in every situation. Your leadership trait will not allow you to fit in everywhere. I know you are a leader because you have influence. You may ask, "How do you know I have influence?" Well, I am certain that someone has done or tried something based on your recommendation. Someone watched a movie or TV show because you said it was awesome. Someone tried a restaurant because you said it was delicious. I can guarantee that you have influenced someone to do something solely based on your suggestion. That is influence and influence is leadership. With that being said, I want to share with you six absolute musts that every volleyball player must have and every leader in life (that is you) must have.

CHARACTER

In volleyball, it is imperative that teammates trust each other. It is necessary that all teammates know that the support of each other is a priority and that they can count on each other. They must be able to trust that every action displayed by a teammate is based on a desire to see the team win. Just like trust is necessary, integrity is necessary. They must know that every teammate is committed to the victory of the team over the recognition of themselves as an individual player. They must know that every teammate considers the team a unified family. There is no real team without players who possess character. In leadership, one cannot be an effective leader and lack character. People must be able to trust you. Trust is built when people can witness your actions line up with your words. Trust is built when people discover somehow that you do the right thing even when no one is watching. Trust is built when people witness you doing the right thing even when doing the wrong thing is not only possible but can be excused, covered up, or explained away. People need to be able to trust you. They need to know that you will follow through with what you say you are going to do. The Bible says in Ecclesiastes 5:5, "It is better not to vow than to vow and not pay." Trust is built when people can rest assured that you are a person of integrity. Being a person of integrity means being an honest person and having a moral standard or set of principles that you govern yourself by. If your character is faulty, nothing else matters. Gifts, talents, abilities, experience, education, resources, or previous successes do not outweigh or outlast integrity. People would much rather follow a less talented person who they can trust over an exceptionally talented person who they cannot trust. If you are going to be a great leader, you must be a person of great character.

CONFIDENCE

Volleyball players must play with confidence. This confidence comes from both courage and certainty. Being certain allows you to be courageous. Therefore, volleyball players must be certain about their roles and responsibilities. They must be certain about their movements and responses. They must be certain about their abilities and knowledge of the game. They must be certain about their strength as a player, and it is critical they are certain about what they bring to the team. This certainty is admirable, contagious, and brings security to the other teammates. No one wants to play with a teammate that is nervous and unsure. No one wants to play with a teammate that is insecure and doubtful about themselves. Mindsets and beliefs are contagious. A powerful team is made up of confident players. As a leader, you must be confident. Even if you are functioning in faith and hope that something will work, you must exude confidence. People do not want to follow an insecure leader. In fact, many companies have experienced massive calamities because of insecure leadership. It is important to note that insecurity is expressed in diverse ways, depending on a person's temperament, values, and conditioned habits. Sometimes insecurity looks like meekness, compliance, and always assuming blame.

Sometimes it looks like overt boldness intended to impress or intimidate others. Sometimes insecurity causes a person to avoid attention at all costs while in others it causes them to demand attention as much as possible. Insecurity cannot be judged based on external actions. Insecurity is based on our awareness or lack thereof of who we are. One is either secure or insecure based on who they believe themselves to be. It is based on our belief of our essential self. It is based on how we see ourselves, our identity. Insecure individuals are individuals who subconsciously acknowledge a threat to their identity. The big question for all of us is, where do we obtain our identity? Our answer to that is the difference between being a secure person or an insecure person. If you find your identity or sense of worth in anything or anyone outside of God, then you will discover that you are an insecure person. Why? People and circumstances change and when they change, our identity and sense of worth will change with them. God remains the same. Therefore, if our sense of worth and identity is found in Him, it will remain solid. When your confidence is connected to God, you will find that you have a quiet, inner knowledge that you are capable. Confidence is a mindset that comes from trusting that when God made you, He made you enough. Embrace your identity in God. You are awesome because He made you awesome. Recognize that you are His masterpiece and walk in confidence. As stated in Chapter 9, note the difference between confidence and arrogance. Arrogance is trust in yourself. Confidence is trust in who God made you. Be confident and be the leader that God has called you to be.

COMMUNICATION

Volleyball players must be excellent communicators both verbally and non-verbally. They must be able to communicate all the non-verbal cues to their teammates. Sometimes it is necessary for a slight body movement or hand gesture to communicate to another player what is to come. Oftentimes, the communication is through a head nod or eye movement. At other times, the communication is obvious and sometimes it is very subtle. There are multiple ways to communicate, but all ways must be direct and clear. Communication is an art. Leaders must master the art of communication. Whenever I talk to couples, I always remind or inform them that communication is approximately 7% content, 38% tone, and 55% non-verbal. Everything that you do overrides everything that you say. Often people will completely miss what you said because they watched what you did. Expressing that you support, love, or care for someone is communicated louder through your body language, hand gestures, and mannerisms than the words coming out of your mouth. Keep this in mind as you seek to grow as a communicator. I have witnessed comedians so gifted that before they even speak a word, people are laughing. I have observed actors so talented that before they utter a line, people are crying. This is because communication occurs mostly through what you are doing and not what you are saying. Practice effective communication and experience growth as a leader.

CONCENTRATION

For volleyball players to maximize their time on the court with their team, they must be focused on what is happening. To concentrate means to focus your attention on a specific object or activity. During the game, the only thing that can be on the player's mind is the game. Everything else must wait until the game is over. To be an effective leader, one must be able to focus. Every environment that we enter is full of multiple elements to focus on. However, a good leader quickly identifies what the focus needs to be. Our focus should always be on the very thing that helps bring success to the project or event on which we are working. Anything that does not help move the agenda for the event or project forward must wait until the completion of the event or project. Several leaders lack optimal success because they lack the ability to remain focused. They have incredible gifts, talents, and abilities, but simply lack the ability to concentrate. One of the weakest kinds of leader is a leader whose mind wanders. Great leaders keep their mind on the current project. I have found that the key to maintaining concentration on any given project is found in one's ability to apply the words of Philippians 4:8: "Finally, brethren, whatever things are true, whatever things are noble, whatever things are just, whatever things are pure, whatever things are lovely, whatever things are of good report, if there is any virtue and if there is anything praiseworthy—meditate on these things." Using this scripture as your template for any endeavor will greatly enhance your ability to concentrate and stay motivated and effective. Amazing leaders know how to concentrate.

CONSIDERATION

Volleyball players have a few key elements that they must consider as they are playing the game. They must consider the game as a whole, they must consider how their actions affect the game, and they must consider what is best for their team as a whole. Players must understand that everything they do does not just affect them, but it affects the entire team. Every action has a reaction; therefore, they must consider the team as they make decisions that will impact the team. In leadership, we must consider how our actions affect everyone around us. Someone is affected by every decision that we make. Sometimes the effects are obvious and oftentimes, the effects go unnoticed for quite a while, but understand that there is always an effect. In the Book of Jonah, we discover that Jonah's disobedience to God brought an entire storm upon a boat full of innocent people. Whatever you do, go out of your way to ensure that innocent people do not have to suffer the negative consequences of your actions. Consider the past, present, and future. Consider your family and friends. Consider the people around you. Before you embark upon a decision, consider the cost. Great leaders are considerate people. Being considerate helps us make selfless decisions instead of selfish decisions. Be a great leader by being a considerate leader.

CONTROL

Volleyball players must know how to control their emotions, reactions, and movements. Additionally, they must know how to control the ball and flow of the game. Control is everything. At the end of the day, the winning team is the team that controlled the game the best. A lack of control is a recipe for chaos and confusion. Leaders must know how to control the environment in which they lead. I did not say manipulate. I said control. There is a dramatic difference. When I speak of control, I am speaking of possessing the ability to manage. Great leaders must be able to manage their emotions, reactions, movements, and overall environment. It takes both security and maturity to do this effectively. Your environment should never be chaotic or full of confusion. You must set a positive atmosphere by being a positive example. Be what you would like to lead. Consider yourself a thermostat and not a thermometer. A thermometer reflects the temperature in the room, but a thermostat sets the temperature in the room. It is the leader's job to set the atmosphere. Whether you are leading in your house or on your job, it is your responsibility to set the atmosphere. Bring the vibe you desire to lead within. As the leader, it is up to you. Master the art of positive, effective control and function as the great leader that God created you to be.

Volleyball holds the secrets to possessing victory in leadership. Apply these principles that I learned from evaluating the game and the players and watch your level of leadership grow to the next level.

A Moment of Reflection
Chapter 10: Life is Like Volleyball: How to Be a Great Leader

As you reflect on how "Life is Like Volleyball," what are your strongest traits as a leader? What are the traits given in this chapter that you need to develop or improve upon?

A Moment of Reflection

A Moment of Reflection

A Moment of Reflection

Chapter 11
LIFE IS LIKE WEIGHTLIFTING: HOW TO EMBRACE RESISTANCE

"Yet in all these things we are more than conquerors through Him who loved us.
- Romans 8:37 (NKJV)

"For by You I can run against a troop, by my God I can leap over a wall."
- Psalm 18:29 (NKJV)

I grew up watching my dad work out and lift weights. In fact, he was so committed to lifting weights that he had a weight bench and set of weights at his job. My dad worked as a sound engineer for a major Hollywood movie studio and would keep a weight bench and set of weights on the actual soundstage. Whenever there was downtime, he would walk onto the soundstage and lift weights. You would have only had to see my dad one time to know that he was serious about weightlifting. His appearance spoke for itself. As a young boy, I saw the benefits of lifting weights. Growing up playing sports, I would spend many days lifting weights. It was not easy, but it was beneficial. I have discovered that the most beneficial actions are usually not the easiest and the easiest actions are usually not the most beneficial. Anyone who has spent time lifting weights, can tell you that it is arduous work but very well worth every effort. As I thought about all that weightlifting entails, I discovered that there is much that we can learn from weightlifting as it pertains to embracing resistance. It is understood that people, in general, do not like resistance. I do not think that I have ever met anyone who likes resistance. In fact, if possible, we will avoid resistance at all costs. Though we understand that resistance is a part of life, we still seek ways around it. However, I believe if we really spent time focusing on and understanding the benefits of resistance, we would appreciate and even embrace it when it arises. I want to give you four aspects of weightlifting and the relationship that it has to this idea of embracing resistance with hope that it will help you better understand the benefits of resistance in your life. I can tell you now that resistance helps you more than it hurts you. That is not to say that it feels good, but rather to say that often it is good.

THE PERCEPTION

As with anything in life, you can personally categorize resistance as either being helpful or hurtful. How you categorize something determines how you approach and appreciate it. When we understand the power and benefits of   resistance in weightlifting, it is easier for us to categorize resistance in life as helpful more than hurtful. Lifting weights with weak effort and weak resistance also supplies deficient productivity and deficient benefit. Such is the same with life. Life without challenges and resistance is usually life without strengths and productivity. Why? Anything of substance must go through a proving process and the best proving process is often a process of resistance. In weightlifting, muscle and strength are built through resistance. I would even go as far to say that determination and focus on weightlifting are both built through resistance. It is the resistance that helps you hit your weightlifting goals. While you can feel as if it is working against you, it is working for you. Life is the same way. Resistance comes to build strength, determination, focus, confidence, and the firmness that is required for success in life.

Your theories and actions must go through the process of someone or something working against them. It is in this process that your theories are proven, and your actions are strengthened. It is through coming out on the other side of this process that you gain courage and determination that can take you from where you are to where you desire to be. Learn to perceive resistance as something working in your favor. From here on, perceive and embrace resistance, not as something trying to stop you, but as something allowed by God to solidify you.

THE PUSH

Whenever you are trying to acquire something, you have never acquired before or accomplish something you have never accomplished before, you will inevitably have to do something you have never done before. Whenever you are lifting weights that you have never lifted before, you will always have to determine that no matter what, you will push through any negative or self-defeating mindset. When you start lifting weights, there will be moments when it seems overwhelming. There will be times when you will not think you can do it and periods when you do not feel it is worth it. Often, you may feel as though you are in over your head. No matter how you feel, remain determined to push past any feeling that is not encouraging you to keep going. Make up in your mind that you are going to push past any feeling of defeat. In life, there are times when you will not want to continue. There will be seasons when you feel defeated, overwhelmed, and like you cannot press forward any further. Push past those feelings. When you push past negative feelings, you discover that not only were they temporary, but they were solely designed to get you to quit. Make up in your mind that as hard as things may be, quitting will never be an option. It may be tough, but do not quit. It may feel overwhelming, but do not quit. You may feel in over your head, but do not quit. If you can push past tough beginnings, you will experience strong endings. The most challenging part is the push that you will have to do in the beginning and making up in your mind that no matter what, you will keep pushing. Push through the resistance and brace yourself for the reward. You embrace resistance by pushing through the negative thoughts connected to the hardest moments in the beginning of the building stages.

THE POWER

In weightlifting, resistance brings power. You gain strength and power through embracing the resistance that comes with the weights that you lifted. In life, resistance brings power. Power is the ability to accomplish something against the odds. When people and circumstances try to stop you and you push past it, you will inevitably gain power. When life brings resistance your way, but you are too determined to let it stop you, you gain power. When people work against you or decide to not collaborate with you at all, and yet you keep going, you gain power. You gain power in your mind. You gain power in your actions. You gain power in your will. When it seems like you are the only one standing, but you are determined to stand, you gain power. Every time you overcome resistance; you gain power. Strong individuals never realize how strong they are until the only option they have is to be strong. Be strong, push through the resistance, and feel the power that shows up in your life.

THE PAIN

Oftentimes, weightlifting brings a certain amount of healthy soreness or pain as you are building muscle and strength. There is a difference between normal and healthy soreness or pain, and abnormal and unhealthy soreness or pain. Knowing this difference helps you determine whether to keep going or adjust and perform a different action. An expected healthy soreness or pain in weightlifting serves as confirmation that your body is responding the way it needs to be responding and that you are growing stronger. In life, there will be periods when resistance will bring an emotional, spiritual, or mental soreness or pain. Meaning, it does not feel pleasant, it is uncomfortable, or it is stretching you beyond your comfort zone. However, understand that there is a purpose in some of the pain that we must experience because of resistance. As is the case with weightlifting, understand the difference between expected and healthy soreness in life and unhealthy soreness in life. The best way to make this determination is to ask yourself, "Is this resistance bringing out the best in me or the worst in me?" Is this situation driving you to give it your all or is it driving you to give up? Is this situation abusive or is it serving as a growing pain? Once you determine that this is just a resistance to bring out the best in you, build and strengthen you, assess your theories, improve your actions, lean into the pain, and watch the process carry you into productivity. Always remember that something can bring out the best in you and yet not be fun or easy. In fact, you can dread going through a certain amount of resistance but determine to go through it because you know it is making you better. The main thing is to be honest about the real potential benefit to hanging in there versus giving up. Do not make decisions based on feelings or emotions because they will mislead you. Evaluate things and make decisions based on whether it is possible for this resistance to make you better eventually. Is sticking with it worth it? Is the long-term benefit one that meets your goal or puts you closer to your goal? Is it pointless to stick with this scenario and do much better going another route?

Weightlifting is not easy, but it can be extremely rewarding. What makes it easier to manage is not the lifting of the weights, but rather the ability to embrace the purpose behind the lifting of the weights. Life is not easy, but life can be extremely rewarding during the process of resistance. What makes the resistance of life easier to manage is embracing purpose behind the process. Understand that resistance can make you better, and not bitter, if you embrace it and understand the purpose behind it.

Allow me to close this chapter with this thought. For some of us, the best thing that has ever happened to us is the fact that we were rejected. Rejection, in many ways, can be categorized as resistance. Rejection does not feel good. No one likes rejection. However, I understand that there is always a purpose behind rejection. For some of us, we would have never disconnected from unhealthy and unproductive people had they not rejected us. Because for some of us, we are so loyal and love so deeply, that we will take even unhealthy people into blessings that they cannot appreciate and will ruin. However, because we will never disconnect from them, it is necessary for God to push them to disconnect from us. That rejection did not feel pleasant, but little did you know it is exactly what you needed to gain strength, power, independence, and a healthy life. Rejection has a way of removing people who no longer need to be there. Anyone who is supposed to be in your life is either already there or on their way. This is one example of how resistance may not look or feel good but works to our advantage.

Learn to embrace resistance through your perception, push, power, and pain and enjoy the long-term benefits connected to that decision.

A Moment of Reflection
Chapter 11: Life is Like Weightlifting: How to Embrace Resistance

As you reflect on how "Life is Like Weightlifting," have you experienced resistance or rejection working in your favor and proving to be a God thing? How?

A Moment of Reflection

A Moment of Reflection

A Moment of Reflection

Chapter 12
LIFE IS LIKE BOWLING: HOW TO STAY OUT OF THE GUTTER

"A wise man fears and departs from evil,
But a fool rages and is self-confident." - Proverbs 14:16 (NKJV)

"A prudent man foresees evil and hides himself, but the simple pass on and
are punished." - Proverbs 22:3 (NKJV)

"The Lord shall preserve your going out and your coming in
From this time forth, and even forevermore." - Psalm 121:8 (NKJV)

If you have ever been or witnessed bowling, you have seen the gutters to the right and left of each bowling lane. Every bowler knows that these gutters are to be avoided at all costs. They are not there to help you in any way, shape, or form. In fact, quite the opposite is true. The gutters are there as an obstacle designed to stop you from hitting your target. If your ball goes into the gutter, that turn is immediately ineffective. The score for a turn that results in the ball going in the gutter is zero. There are zero advantages to the gutter. Nothing productive in them and nothing good comes from them. They only exist to stop you. When we start comparing bowling to life, we must first define what the gutter is in our lives. What are the obstacles in our lives that only exist to stop us? What are the elements that have proven to be unproductive? What are the factors that have never and could never work to our advantage? These are what we need to categorize as the gutters of life and what we need to intentionally stay away from. As I studied the game of bowling, I discovered four formidable tips on how to stay out of the gutters in the bowling lane. Coincidently, these same tips can be applied to our lives and help us stay out of the gutters of life. Staying out of the "gutters of life" starts with knowing the difference between something designed to move you forward and make you better versus something designed to stop you from moving forward and make you bitter. What stops you from moving forward and leaves you feeling bitter is the gutter.

FOCUS FORWARD

There are three key elements you need to focus on, they are: where you are, where you need to be, and what gets you there. Anything that does not get you there can officially be categorized as the gutter. I am a very black and white person. There are no gray areas for me. As I have stated a few times throughout this book, I believe things either help you or hurt you. There is no in-between. Actions or matters are either productive or unproductive. In bowling, your ball is either in the lane or in the gutter. In life, you are either walking in a productive lane or in the gutter. Make up in your mind that you are going to draw clear and strong lines between what is helpful and what is hurtful. If you are struggling to categorize something as one or the other, let me tell you what I do. Jesus declared in John 10:10, "The thief does not come except to steal, and to kill, and to destroy. I have come that they may have life, and that they may have it more abundantly." Based on that scripture, I take a piece of paper and I draw a line down the middle and a line across the top, so it looks like a giant lowercase "t." On the top of the left side, I write "LIFE." On the top of the right side, I write "KILL, STEAL, DESTROY." I then make a list of all the things that bring life from a particular event, situation, person, or circumstance. On the opposite side I make a list of everything that kills, steals, or destroys anything in my life in association with a particular event, situation, person, or circumstance. The longer side is the side that determines whether this event, situation, person, or circumstance is to be kept or disconnected from. My focus remains with the situations that give me life. The situations that do not produce life, immediately lose my time, effort, and focus. As a result, I focus on things that move my life forward. Life is too short to not focus forward by drawing clear lines between what is helpful and what is not helpful.]

USE BUMPERS (MAKE IT POSSIBLE)

I love the fact that, as an option, you can remove the gutters in bowling. Oftentimes, when people know that their ball is going to go into the gutter, they will cover the gutters with bumpers and completely remove them as an option. This is a huge lesson that we can apply to our lives. Some things and even some people need to be removed as options. If some things are options, they will also be temptations. Being that we are responsible for the decisions that we make with our lives, it is our responsibility to remove unproductive options and temptations. People will not remove these unproductive or counter productive options for you. You must be determined to remove them for yourself. Determine that your life is too important and too short to waste time with unproductive or counterproductive things. Determine that you value your life too much to lend it to unproductivity. Time is precious, and once it is gone, it cannot be regained. You are responsible for what dominates your time. Treasure your time. Guard your time. Protect your time. Be mindful of the time that you give to moments that bring you joy, peace, happiness, and fun. Be mindful of the time that you give to work and building success. Conversely, be mindful of the time that you give to irritation, anger, and jealousy. You only have enough time in life to perform all that drives you and the vision that God has given you forward. If you feel drawn away to something or someone that does not drive you or your vision forward, determine a method to place a bumper there so that it becomes impossible to lure you in. Setting up a bumper may look like removing certain contacts from your phone, ending certain relationships, displaying accountability in certain areas of your life, or drastically changing certain habits that you have grown accustomed to but know are either unproductive or counterproductive. To set up a bumper means to put something in place that prohibits you from going into an unproductive or counterproductive area of your life. Set items in place to make it impossible to go into the gutter.

SELECT THE RIGHT WEIGHT

Sometimes the issue with a bowler is that they have simply selected a ball of the wrong weight. As a result, it hinders their ability to properly bowl. Bowling with the wrong weight makes it increasingly difficult to bowl correctly. The wrong weight affects form, approach, style, and overall effectiveness. Some bowlers do not realize that they would have a much better game if they would just use the proper size ball. They do not understand that it matters how much weight you are carrying as you are trying to bowl. Coincidentally, many times, the same is true with life. Too many of us are lured away into temptations or unproductive distractions simply because we are not carrying the proper amount of weight in our lives. The weight can either be too little or too much. When you are not carrying enough weight, your free time or idle time will present temptations or distractions that you do not need to give your time and attention to. The Bible talks about how Satan loves to take advantage of our free time. Sometimes we have too much free time because we are not carrying enough weight in our lives. In other words, we are not occupied enough. On the other hand, sometimes we are carrying too much weight and experience weariness, burnout, frustration, worry, or emotional overload and because of desiring relief from these areas, we are mistakenly drawn into situations that provide temporary relief with long-term damage. Carrying too much is dangerous because when we are completely depleted emotionally, spiritually, and physically, it has a negative effect on our ability to make wise and productive decisions. Do not overwhelm yourself with work. Determine what the proper amount of weight is for you to carry. This is determined by being very honest about both your strengths and your weaknesses. Know if you can manage more, but also know if you are managing too much because every individual is different. Do not base your workload on someone else's workload. We are not in competition with each other. We are individuals who all have a calling in this life. Your workload is your workload, and someone else's workload is their workload. Whatever you do, do not suffer from what I call "comparisonitis." Comparisonitis is making moves in your life based on the moves you see someone else making in their life. It is a terrible tool that Satan uses to pause true and authentic progress. Stay true to yourself and move forward carrying the amount of work (weight) that best fits who God made you to be.

HAVE THE RIGHT APPROACH

Approach matters. With over six billion people on this planet, no two people have the same fingerprint. Do you know what that means? No matter how many people you encounter, you are still one of a kind. You are the only you that exists. Diamonds are expensive because they are rare, but you are priceless because you are the only one. With that being said, your approach to life must be uniquely tailored to the makeup that God has given you. Bowlers understand that they must find their style and their approach to the game. Just because it worked for one bowler does not mean it works for every bowler. Your mindset to your life must be the same. You must find the approach to life that works or you. Just because a certain strategy worked for one individual does not mean it works for every individual. Be secure and comfortable in your personality, your genetic design, and your complete God-given makeup. When you are comfortable being you, you do not search to copy anyone else. Discover what excites you, what motivates you, what drives you to work until you win. Your approach to life is exactly that, your approach to life. The best advice that I can give you is this, spend some alone time with God and ask Him to download into you His approach for your life. The way you do something will determine how well something is done by you. Trust God to give you His way for your life. The gutter is not for you. Success is for you. Winning is for you. Progress and productivity are for you. Apply these four tips that I learned from bowling into your life and watch any potential gutters fade away from your life.

Let this Psalm be the prayer that guards your life and keeps you out of the gutter:

"I will lift up my eyes to the hills—
From whence *comes* my help?
2 My help comes from the Lord,
Who made heaven and earth.
3 He will not allow [my] foot to be moved;
He who keeps [me] will not slumber.
4 Behold, He who keeps Israel

Shall neither slumber nor sleep.
5 The Lord *is* [my] keeper;
The Lord *is* [my] shade at [my] right hand.
6 The sun shall not strike [me] by day,
Nor the moon by night.
7 The Lord shall preserve [me] from all evil;
He shall preserve [my] soul.
8 The Lord shall preserve [my] going out and [my] coming in
From this time forth, and even forevermore."
Psalm 121:1-8 (NKJV)

I personalized this prayer to make it personal for you. Stay out of the gutter.

A Moment of Reflection
Chapter 12: Life is Like Bowling: How to Stay Out of The Gutter

As you reflect on how "Life is Like Bowling," have you been able to identify any issue or factor that has proven to be unproductive and not lend to your success in life at all? What practical steps will you take to make sure that this does not derail your progress and send you into the gutter?

A Moment of Reflection

A Moment of Reflection

A Moment of Reflection

Chapter 13
LIFE IS LIKE HOCKEY: HOW TO KEEP MOVING FORWARD IN LIFE

"Let your eyes look straight ahead, and your eyelids look right before you."
- Proverbs 4:25 (NKJV)

"Before I formed you in the womb, I knew you; Before you were born, I sanctified you; I ordained you a prophet to the nations."
- Jeremiah 1:5 (NKJV)

"For I know the thoughts that I think toward you, says the Lord, thoughts of peace and not of evil, to give you a future and a hope."
- Jeremiah 29:11 (NKJV)

Hockey is truly a distinctive sport. It is incredibly fast-paced, high energy, exhilarating, and intense. It provides an indescribable adrenaline rush for both players and fans. From the slap shots to the cheap shots that lead to fighting, hockey tends to have something for everyone. I am always amazed at how many different skills are required to effectively play the game. While there are many qualities that contribute to one being a great hockey player, there are three main things about the game that I have applied to my life which have helped me repeatedly move forward in life. Life is all about moving forward. You are either moving forward, moving backwards, or not moving at all. Eventually, not moving at all equates to moving backwards because life moves forward whether you move with it or not. Life is all about being further down the road today than you were yesterday and being further down the road tomorrow than you will be by the end of the day today. If we are going to live a life that is constantly moving forward, we must apply these three tips that I have learned from hockey to our daily lives.

SKATING

A great hockey player is a phenomenal skater. They are a phenomenal skater for several reasons, one being the fact that they know how to stay on their feet during such a fast-paced game. Even when they fall, which is inevitable, they know how to get right back up. Another reason they are phenomenal skaters is because they know how to skate and stay ready for action. In other words, they know how to move forward while remaining alert. They understand that being able to remain alert while moving forward during a fast-paced game means knowing how to make last-minute adjustments, shifts, turns, and can stop on a dime. When needed, they can shift and go in another direction, adjust their speed, and navigate through and around obstacles. Such is the same with moving forward in life. Life can be, not only fast paced, but filled with obstacles and situations that call for quick thinking and adjustment. In life, we must learn how to stay on our feet. Chances are great that at some point, you will fall, but that is expected and ok. Just do not stay down. Get back up. I discussed this concept in Chapter 6: Life is Like Soccer. Falling is never a problem. Staying down is a problem. Stay on your feet and move forward putting one foot in front of the other. Baby steps are always better than no steps at all. As you navigate forward in life, know when to stop, know when to adjust, know when to go in a different direction, know when to be flexible, know how to navigate through obstacles that may stand in your way. As you move forward in life, remain alert. Always prepare for what is expected and to the best of your ability, what is unexpected. There is an old quote that states, "If you stay ready, you won't have to get ready." To the best of your ability, stay ready for whatever life may bring your way. You stay ready by staying informed and staying engaged. There is always something to learn and there is always something to connect to. As you move forward in life, you will never run out of information or individuals to help you. Continue moving forward in life. You only miss the needed information and the needed individuals when you stop moving forward.

SANGUINE

Sanguine may be a brand-new vocabulary word for you. It was for me. Sanguine means to be optimistic or positive, especially in a terrible or difficult situation. No matter how good the other team is, or what the score may be, a skilled hockey player knows that you must remain optimistic. Attitude is everything. If you do not think you can, then you cannot. However, if you think you can, you can. Your attitude determines your atmosphere, your atmosphere determines your actions, and your actions determine your advancement toward your desired achievement. No matter what life brings your way, remember there is always something to smile about and work toward. There is always something to celebrate. There is always something from which to draw motivation. For all the dreadful things that did happen, there is always a gratefulness to be felt for the things that did not happen. For all the good things that did not happen, there is always gratefulness to be felt for all the dreadful things that did not happen. At any given point in your life, you can rest assured that you have more going for you than you have going against you. While it can be tempting to focus on everything that is not going right, choose to constantly remind yourself of everything that is going right. Stay encouraged. I do not even have to know you personally to know that you have a story of survival. You have a story of overcoming. You have a story of coming out on the other side of what should have destroyed you. Do you know why you have a history of overcoming, surviving, winning, and making it out of terrible situations? It is because God's Hand is on your life, and He will never leave or forsake you. You have never been by yourself. In Matthew 1:20-23, "An angel of the Lord" appeared to Joseph in a dream, after he discovered that his betrothed, soon-to-be wife, the virgin Mary was pregnant with child, to remind him, "That which is conceived in her is of the Holy Spirit" and also to remind him of the words spoken by the Prophet Isaiah in Isaiah 7:14, "Behold, the virgin shall conceive and bear a Son, and they shall call His name Immanuel." The angel then explains that Immanuel is translated, "God with us." I want to remind you that God is not above us like nature will try to teach us. God is not against us like the law of religion will try to teach us. Rather, God is with us, like the angel taught us through what he told Joseph regarding his situation. You must know and believe that God is with you now and forevermore. Since God is with you, hold your head up, square your shoulders, and know that no weapon formed against you is going to prosper. Be encouraged, knowing that God is on your side. He created you to win. Oftentimes, God will send us through situations that look like they are going to destroy us. However, He will bring us through it so that we and everyone around us will know that anything and everything can be overcome with Him on our side. If God brings you to it, He will most certainly bring you through it. Stay motivated and remember that at the end of the day, whatever battles you face are not yours to face alone. They are yours to give to God and watch Him work it out with you and for you. Keep your head up and keep going with a positive and faith-filled attitude. Someone once said, "You have to fake it until you make it." That is not good advice. Instead, because we have God with us, I say, "You have to faith it until you make it." Faith forward and keep going.

STICK HANDLING

One of the golden rules of hockey is to keep your stick on the ice. This means staying engaged in the game. You never know when the puck is going to come your way. The worst thing that can happen is that the puck comes your way, and you miss it because your stick was not on the ice. Too many of us pray for blessings that we are not ready to receive. Keeping your stick on the ice means staying engaged and staying ready so that when "the puck," opportunity, or answer to your prayer comes your way, you will not miss it because you were distracted and not engaged. You never know when God is going to send an opportunity your way. Remain ready to receive. If God were to give you a yes to your prayer request today, would you truly be ready to receive it? Perhaps you would, but if there is any part of you that knows that you are not fully ready to receive, do everything within your power to be positioned for the yes to your prayer request. Keeping your stick on the ice means staying involved. You cannot disconnect from life and expect to be positioned to receive God's blessings in life. The Bible expresses messages about persevering even when you want to give up. The Bible says that, if you persevere, there is a time appointed for what you have been waiting for to finally show up. Do not miss it because you gave up too soon. Do not miss it because you walked away too soon. Do not miss it because you grew impatient. Do not miss it because you checked out. Keep your stick on the ice. The Bible admonishes us to keep going while seizing and maximizing every moment that comes our way. Keep your hand to the plow. Your labor is not in vain. Your hard work is not in vain. The Bible declares in Habakkuk 2:3a, "For the vision is yet for an appointed time…" Now is not the time to break down. Now is the time to break through so that you can break out and break free into the big break that God has appointed for you.

Here is a quick note regarding stickhandling. Excellent hockey players know the importance of passing the puck. Sometimes the best decision they can make is to pass the puck knowing that in this situation, it is better to release it and give it to someone who is in a better position to do something with it. In life, it is wise to know when it is time to pass something to someone else. As much as we like to hold on and go for the score, we must know when to go for it and when to pass it to someone who is in a better position to do something with it. Remember, a team win is always better than an individual accomplishment. At times, we grasp on too long because we say, "God told me to do this." Unfortunately, we can be so caught up on what God told us, that we miss what He is currently telling us. God may have told you to manage something for a season, not for a lifetime.

These three quick tips from hockey have helped me countless times continue moving forward in life when it seemed like life tried everything within its power to pause my progression. Apply these tips to your life and keep moving forward.

A Moment of Reflection
Chapter 13: Life is Like Hockey: How to Keep Moving Forward in Life

As you reflect on how "Life is Like Hockey," how easy has it been for you to continue moving forward in life? What can you implement into your life today that makes moving forward even easier? How can you ensure that every tomorrow is better than the day before?

A Moment of Reflection

A Moment of Reflection

A Moment of Reflection

Chapter 14
LIFE IS LIKE WRESTLING: HOW TO SEE THE GOOD IN WHAT SEEMS BAD

"Weeping may endure for a night, but joy comes in the morning."
- Psalm 30:5b (NKJV)

"Keep your heart with all diligence, for out of it spring the issues of life."
- Proverbs 4:23 (NKJV)

"Do not be anxious about anything, but in every situation, by prayer and petition, with thanksgiving, present your requests to God. And the peace of God, which transcends all understanding, will guard your hearts and your minds in Christ Jesus. Finally, brothers and sisters, whatever is true, whatever is noble, whatever is right, whatever is pure, whatever is lovely, whatever is admirable— if anything is excellent or praiseworthy—think about such things. Whatever you have learned or received or heard from me or seen in me—put it into practice. And the God of peace will be with you."
- Philippians 4:6-9 (NIV)

Wrestling is quite intense and requires a great deal of courage, resilience, and consistency; not to mention, strength and wisdom. Being that it is a strenuous contact sport and requires you to always be more proactive (going on the attack) than reactive (waiting for the attack), there is a great deal that can be learned from wrestling as it relates to managing this life, in which Jesus says will present trials, tests, and seasons of tribulation. Skilled wrestlers will agree that the match is won or lost in the mind before it is won or lost on the mat. Perception carries power. If you want to have power over any given circumstance, that power lies in your perception of that circumstance. There is an old psychological question stating, "Is the glass half empty or is it half full?" Your power in life lies in your response being solidified in the fact that the glass is always half full. Life can be quite challenging at times. However, life always has opportunities for growth and advancement. Your ability to recognize and see these moments will again lie in your life's motto being some variation of the statement that the glass is always half full. What I love about wrestling is that it teaches us how to see the positive in situations that seem to only be detrimental. There are five things that I learned from observing and studying wrestling that I want to share with you in hopes that it will help you forever see how there is always good in what is bad.

OWN YOUR LIFE

No matter how large the coaching staff or supporting list of individuals may be behind any particular wrestler, when it comes down to it, wrestling is an individual sport. When it is go time, the wrestler must take to the mat by themselves. Their coaches cannot wrestle for them. Their team of people cannot wrestle for them. Their supporters cannot wrestle for them. When it is all said and done, they must wrestle for themselves. In life, we must understand that it is up to us to own our life. This is perhaps some of the greatest news you could ever receive. Do you know what it truly means to own your life? It means that you have complete control of your responses and of the power and influence that people have over your life. Consider your life as a Major Motion Picture. God has given you the power to be the producer, writer, star, director, and casting agent. This means that people function in the roles that you assign to them, and they carry the power that you assign to that specific role. This is great news because this means that you carry the power to send your life into whatever direction you want your life to go into. Your greatest enemy will always be your inner me. You can change the course of your life today if you want to. You can choose to remove yourself from people who are holding you back or holding you down. This is your life, and it is up to you and only you to set the course for it. You determine what will stop you. You determine what will depress you. You determine what will hold you back. You determine what will slow you down. You determine what will destroy you. You determine what will crush you. You determine what will control you. Even if you make a drastic change for the better and it seems like things worsen, understand that skyscrapers are built going down into the ground before they are built going up. They are built going down so that the foundation can be strong. The higher up they are going to be built, the further down they must go first. Why do they have to go down before they go up? When the skyscraper is complete, should there be an earthquake, tornado, hurricane or major storm, the building may sway, but it will not fall. Never let having to downsize, restart, regroup, or reboot discourage you because it is better to start fresh with a solid foundation than continue in something that is not helping you maximize your gifts, talents, and abilities in life. Own your life and own your future.

SCORE FROM THE BOTTOM

Unbelievably, if your opponent has you pinned to the mat in wrestling, you can still score. You can score by breaking or escaping your opponent's grasp. You can also score in a major way if you execute a reversal. A reversal means you transition from being on bottom to being on top. Every now and then, a coach will have an unusually wise strategy for a wrestler to get on the bottom and score points. To someone who does not know much about wrestling, it seems wrong for a wrestler to incorporate being on bottom into the strategy for winning. However, an experienced wrestler knows that there are points to be gained from the bottom. In life, sometimes the bottom is the best place to be because the only place from there is up. In some cases, the bottom presents a wonderful opportunity to lay a new foundation or start fresh. Sometimes the bottom presents wonderful opportunities for gaining new information, resources, connections, or insight. The bottom sometimes slows us down so that we can put together a solid strategy for moving up. The good news about the bottom is that you cannot go down any further and that you have officially survived the absolute worst that could possibly happen. The bottom is actually proof that you are an overcomer and conqueror. Instead of being depressed by the bottom, find encouragement and courage in the fact that you are now headed up. Use this as an opportunity to align yourself with everything needed to gain everything that you desire. Utilize the bottom as an opportunity to climb to your destination of choice one move at a time. The bottom is not the end of your story. It is the end of the worst of your story. It is an official beginning to the best of your story. The bottom is a new birth or re-birth; like a launching pad that propels you right back to the top. Make the most of the bottom and rise to the place that you desire to be.

INJURIES ARE LESSONS

I have never met a wrestler that says they love injuries, but I have met plenty of wrestlers who say that injuries have given them wonderful lessons. Even if they do not know what to do, an injury is always a reminder of what not to do. In life, we will experience injuries. They are not fun. I have never met anyone who says that they enjoy the injuries of life. However, just like in wrestling, the injuries of life carry powerful lessons that can produce many victories in life. From every injury that you may experience, ask yourself, "What is the lesson that this injury is trying to impart into me?" That lesson is one of your keys to success. Everything in life carries a lesson. When we are injured by life, we have a major choice to make. We can choose to get knocked down and stay down, or we can muster up enough strength to get up and ask ourselves, "What lesson is couched in this injury that can help make me better and bring me another step closer to my preferred present and future?" Nobody likes pain, but pain has great power when we use it to gain something productive within ourselves. May every injury unlock a lesson and ignite something on the inside of you that drives you far beyond your happiest and most joyful memory in life. Learn the lesson and move forward in the wisdom of that lesson.

EVERY FIGHT IS TEMPORARY

Wrestling matches do not last forever, though they may seem like they do for the wrestlers involved, they are all temporary. Nothing in life is forever. The good, the bad, and the ugly are all temporary. Knowing this gives us the strength that we need to get through every situation. As challenging as situations may get, know that it is temporary. The Bible is clear in Psalm 30:5b that, "Weeping may endure for a night, but joy comes in the morning." The Bible clearly states that there are seasons assigned to everything. Therefore, your rough times are temporary. Your tough times are temporary. Your most trying times are temporary. No matter your life's circumstances, which are negative or discouraging, they are all temporary. The fight is not forever. The struggle is not forever. I will go as far to say that the time frame for the seasons of difficulty depends on the decisions you make during that season of your life. The time frame depends on your attitude during that season. In many ways, the time frame is up to you. Make seasons of difficulty as short as possible by being determined and confident in making consistent moves to bring positive change into your life.

THERE IS ALWAYS A WAY OUT

I have seen wrestlers escape scenarios that I thought they would never be able to get out of. I have seen situations that seemed impossible for a wrestler to escape, yet somehow, they managed to not only escape, but come out on top and win the match. I have seen wrestlers shock everyone with how they managed to win a match that they were losing the entire time. Every time I see this scenario play out, it reminds me of the fact that no matter what position we find ourselves in with life, there is always a way out. There is always a way of escape. There is always a way to turn that situation around, come out on top, and ultimately win. Do not ever think that you are without a way to win, come out on top, or reverse everything that is going against you. With God on your side, you can overcome anything. Remember, you are always one game plan or strategy away from turning your life completely around and having everything work in your favor. Success is always possible. In this moment, you are connected to a solution that will bring you the life you have always wanted. Remember, you will not see the answers while seeing the glass as half empty because the match is won in the mind before it is won on the mat. Understand that when God created an entrance to the most difficult seasons of your life, He also created an exit. Seek Him for that exit and enter the best days of your life.

In every unpleasant situation in your life, there is far more good waiting to be discovered. The good always outweighs the bad. See the good in what seems bad and move forward in that revelation.

A Moment of Reflection
Chapter 14: Life is Like Wrestling: How to See the Good in What Seems Bad

As you reflect on how "Life is Like Wrestling," how have the tools given in this chapter helped you see the good in what once only seemed bad?

A Moment of Reflection

A Moment of Reflection

A Moment of Reflection

Upcoming Book Release

"Winning In The Most Unlikely Places"

Booking Info

Request@PastorMarlon.com
www.PastorMarlon.com
www.hopecitycolorado.com
Hope City Phone Number – (720) 710-9535
Mailing Address
6140 S. Gun Club Road #K6-276
Aurora, CO 80016
Stay Connected on Social Media
www.facebook.com/pastormarlon
www.instagram.com/marlonsaunders

The Saunders Family

Jaymie Cocas (Alexander) Jaymies Touch Photography